"Chandra's joy and enthusiasm are irrepressible and irresistible. She completely redefines what it means to be a Church Lady and challenges us all to embrace the calling to take the church into the world. After studying this book, you will find your inner Church Lady!"

—JENNIFER KENNEDY DEAN, the Praying Life Foundation, best-selling author of *Live a Praying Life*

"Do you consider yourself a Church Lady? If you're a believer in Jesus Christ, then you are! In her book, *Church Lady*, Chandra Peele tears down the old stereotype and breaks through preconceptions by painting a beautiful portrait of the Church Lady like God sees her. You will laugh, cry, cheer, and perhaps cringe as Chandra illustrates biblical truth through the stories of Church Ladies she has encountered all across the globe. She also personally and transparently shares her own journey to become the Church Lady God desires her to be. You will be encouraged. You will be challenged. But more importantly, you'll find the freedom to be the Church Lady God designed you to be."

—KATHY HOWARD, author of *Unshakeable Faith: 8 Traits for Rock-Solid Living*

"I love this lady. She always makes me laugh and cry. Two special gifts to my life. This book speaks truth to those walking a journey with Christ. The reader will be richer and deeper from the read."

—ESTHER BURROUGHS, director of Esther Burroughs Ministries, speaker, and author

Church

LADY

FREED *to* BE *a* WOMAN *of* GOD

LADY

CHANDRA PEELE

NEW HOPE
PUBLISHERS
BIRMINGHAM, ALABAMA

New Hope® Publishers
P. O. Box 12065
Birmingham, AL 35202-2065
www.NewHopeDigital.com
New Hope Publishers is a division of WMU®.

Library of Congress Cataloging-in-Publication Data Library of Congress Cataloging-in-Publication Data

Peele, Chandra.
  Church lady : freed to be a woman of God.
    p. cm.
  ISBN 978-1-59669-323-4 (sc)
  1. Christian women--Religious life. I. Title.
  BV4527.P398 2012
  248.8'43--dc23

                      2011045860

ISBN-10: 1-59669-323-1
ISBN-13: 978-1-59669-323-4

N124130 · 0312 · 3M1

Dedication

With greatest joy I dedicate this book to
The Cherished Chicks

*Nine godly, crazy, fun, beautiful, REAL Church Ladies
who demonstrate the genuine love Paul describes in Romans 12
every day of their lives.*

While others I have met along this journey may not be in the official group of nine, you should be!

During my ten-year journey in search of the Church Lady:

When I was lonely, you called me.

When I was struggling, you prayed for me.

When I was mourning, you supported me.

When I needed girl time, you made it happen.

When I needed a hand to help and a shoulder to lean on, you offered yours.

When I needed to cry, you cried with me. When I needed to laugh, you gave me reason.

We've been with each other through the ups and downs; the good times and the not-so-good times; and even the really, really not-so-good times.

We've celebrated birthdays, graduations, anniversaries, weddings, and life together.

We've worshipped and praised God together. We've prayed together and stayed together.

Cherished Chicks, you represent our heavenly Father well!

You are the Church Lady every woman longs to have as a friend.

You are a blessing to me and you've brought me much joy!

I cherish your friendship and I love you dearly!

Now for every Church Lady whose story is found in this book, who listened to the stories, who prayed for me, planned a retreat, or gave me an opportunity to speak—you, too, are a Cherished Chick.

May we continue to be the church—His daughters, stepping out and shining bright as we proclaim the good news—the love of Jesus Christ.

Cherished—held dear; treated with care and affection; kept deeply in mind

Chicks—Women

Contents

Acknowledgments

Collecting. We all collect something: antiques, silver spoons, purses, a certain type of object (for me it's vintage plates). We collect friends, experiences, and memories even if we aren't conscious of this. If we look closely, each of us has a theme that manifests itself in our lives. The choices and decisions made in our mind—woven together—become the passion of our hearts. Mixed together, these determine the role we play on the stage of our lives.

In fact, for many years now I've been collecting the stories of Church Ladies and I've been passionate about it. On the journey, I realized I had taken some things for granted. The sweet, sweet spirit received from the body of believers; the sense of family we share with complete strangers because of Christ in us; and the sisterhood I have with Church Ladies—from my next-door neighbor to new friends on the other side of the world! Each one unique, each one with a story, each one my sister, and each one God has used to weave a thread through the pages of this book.

While some have simply brushed by me for a moment, others have supported me from the very beginning and will celebrate the release of Church Lady as if I've just delivered a baby! Although there's not enough room to name each one who has touched my life on this journey, I can't pass by an opportunity to acknowledge some.

To Lindsey and Holly, my daughters—You were the first to hear the vision. In fact, you've heard about Church Lady more than half your life now. Thank you for letting me use your stories and for always being my greatest cheerleaders. There is no greater joy for a mama Church Lady than to watch her daughters become Church Ladies too! I love you both dearly!

To my mom—Thank you for being my first example of a Church Lady. So much of you is woven into me. Thank you for always believing God would—when I could not. Thank you for believing the vision from the moment I shared it with you till now. It's finally finished!

To Melissa, my almost twin (little) sister—Two things that are certain, whether on the mountaintop or to the lowest place in the valley, no matter where life takes us we're there for each other. And although I've been transparent on the pages of this book, the truth is, no one knows a sister like a sister.

Denalyn, Diane, Margie, and Alisa—Thank you for being my forever friends! It's so true that those who pray together stay together. I love you and praise God for you. Your love, kindness, giving, prayer, and always believing He would work through me (when some did not) . . . is priceless!

Leslie—You've heard the stories, read them before anyone else, supported me, prayed for me, cooked for my family, and the list goes on and on. It's been a sweet season, one I'm so glad I've collected along the journey.

Cyndi Blau—When God moved us back to Houston, I was thankful He had you directly in my path. From the first moment we met you've been my sista! Thank you for the time you've given this ministry, this book, and for your gift of serving. You are such a blessing to me and my family.

To Andrea Mullins—one of the finest Church Ladies I know—What a privilege to work with you! Thank you for believing in the vision and waiting for the Lord's direction and timing for this project. It takes a village and I'm so glad New Hope lives in mine.

Joyce Dinkins—Thank you for the wisdom, laughs, and "atta girls" all when I need them most! Thank you for being a bright spot in the aisle of Church Ladies. Love you!

Ashley Stephens—Thank you for taking care of all the details so I don't have to and for being so sweet as you serve.

To the New Hope Team—You're the best! Thank you for every part you play to get books from God's inspiration, from the manuscript, to the printed pages, to ebooks, and to the eyes of the reader.

To Bruce—my wonderful husband and one of the finest Church Men I know—Thank you for believing this is the book I was made to write and one God will use to bless His daughters, Church Ladies all over the world. Thank you for always believing in me and for loving me with a genuine love (Romans 12).

To you—the reader—Thank you for picking this book up. Thank you for sharing it with your friends. Stay strong, be joyful, and love like you've never loved before. You are His radiant bride! You are the Church Lady! Together we stand, together we live, and together we shine the wonderful name of Jesus!

Father God, to You I give the most honor and glory. For it was You who gave the vision and the inspiration to write. It is You who took me on the journey, who opened doors of opportunity, and who winked when You were ready for me to share it with the world. Thank You, Lord! It is my joy and honor to serve You. I pray that You have bigger plans for this book than I can imagine and that the simple but real stories will resonate Your love to all those who read the words. The book is for You, Lord. Thank You for the privilege of writing it.

Foreword

I've known Chandra for almost 20 years. Our girls were 7 years old and they are 25 and 26 now. She was new to San Antonio and our girls were in the same second-grade class. They became fast friends and so did we. It's pretty hard to not like Chandra. She is Miss Bubbles. Besides that, we have a lot in common which made our friendship fun. Even now we can go months without talking and then pick up where we left off.

One of the things I admire most about Chandra is her gift of faith. I know we all have faith, but she has the gift of faith. In my study of this gift, I learned this person has a supernatural ability to believe God for things beyond the ordinary and without this gift there would be no vision. Well, my friend Chandra believes God, and He gives her visions in her spirit, including at night when she sleeps.

Church Lady or unchurched lady, you will be blessed as Chandra shares what God has shown her, taught her, and done in her. As you read, you will feel like she is your best friend taking you on a great road trip. This trip will be insightful as you see yourself in the Church Lady. You will stop along the way and visit many friends; one is a free spirit who worships God unimpeded, another is full of tattoos and Jesus, and one has a love of hospitality and encourages others. But what they and we have in common on this journey of life is a relationship with our Father God, Jesus Christ, and the Holy Spirit.

God is making this road we travel into a wedding aisle, preparing His bride, the church, for His return. This preparation will include visits to the valley and mountaintop euphoria and lots of flatland in between. In Church Lady, Chandra openly and honestly shares about this journey on which we find ourselves. She also casts vision for us, speaking truth from God's Word, His road map for us.

The goal for our journey is to experience God in all of it—the good and the bad, with the victories and defeats.

God is in the travel business and He knows perfectly well how to get us from point A to point B and ultimately from earth to heaven, from dust to divine, from one degree of glory to the next.

Chandra is the tour guide in this book, but she knows the One who created the mountains and the valleys and the flatlands. She does a great job of walking us closer to Him, so close that He can speak into our hearts and tell us who we are. And if we will believe Him, we will mount up with wings like the eagle. We will run and not grow weary and we will walk and not faint.

Now that's what I call a good trip.

So sit back, relax with your favorite travel mug, and enjoy the journey of the Church Lady.

Denalyn Lucado

Introduction

Here is the church, here is the steeple.
Open the door and see all the people.

— NURSERY RHYME

ou've seen her. You may even *be* her — the godly and beautiful woman who, in spite of herself, has resembled her complete opposite twin, evil and ugly, a time or two in her life. And wouldn't you know it? That was the exact moment someone snapped a picture and recorded it on the hard drive of her mind, filed it under Stereotypes, and titled it "Church Lady." Most will agree that even we, God's daughters, have helped to keep this infamous stereotype alive, pointing to this person or that, proclaiming that *"she is the Church Lady, certainly not me!"*

Somewhere along the way, this woman of noble character (wholesome, God-fearing, lovable, kind, giving, and serving) has lost her respect. I say it's time for a do-over, a truce, a meeting of the sisters. Let's delete the hard drive, wipe out the negative stereotype, and shine up her tarnished reputation. Let's reclaim the honor and humility that is the Church Lady.

What about you? What comes to your mind when you think of the all-too-familiar Church Lady? Much to my surprise, these two words carry a lot of weight, as they reference many character traits and have evolved through the ages.

STEREOTYPE — *I'm not old enough to be called a Church Lady.*
For some women, the words *Church Lady* are how they describe the sweet elderly woman who has sat on the third pew in her church as long as they can remember. She wears a suit, pantyhose, modestly heeled dress shoes, and a fancy hat. She has her hair fixed at the beauty shop on Saturday (sleeps with a scarf to protect it), so she looks her very best for worship on Sunday morning. She knows everything about the Bible (at least that's what you think), prays with *Thee* and *Thou*, and always has a kind word to say.

STEREOTYPE — *I'm not good enough to be called a Church Lady.*
For other women, the Church Lady represents those ladies who come every summer to share Bible stories that tell of Jesus, God's Son, the Savior of the world. She's the one who brings spiritual and physical food, new clothes, shoes, a blanket for our beds, and always a smile and a hug.

STEREOTYPE — *I don't want to be called a Church Lady!*
Unfortunately for others, hearing the words *Church Lady* immediately takes them back to one they have known who was judgmental and legalistic, stuffy and religious — a Church Lady who looked down on others as she sat high upon her self-righteous throne.

Oh, sister! Let's not allow these stereotypes to exist a moment longer. There are many Church Ladies who are godly and beautiful from the inside out — those who are *real,* who shine the love of Christ in their homes, their communities, their nation, and their world. Those of us who believe in the one true God are aware that we are called to love, to show kindness, to stand up for the truth, to serve others, and to be the hands and feet of Jesus while here on this earth. Do we make mistakes? You betcha, but it's certainly not intentional, and it's not without regret. So how do we change this negative stereotype? We redefine it — we redefine the Church Lady.

First we need to look at our hearts. If we are honest, we need to admit that not a day goes by when something we hear or see prompts us to form opinions about others. After all, isn't it our own insecurity — and perhaps fear — that causes us to make negative assumptions of others? If someone is different than we are, we instinctively put up a protective shield, and our spontaneous thoughts often cause knee-jerk reactions that reveal our true colors, and often our ugly thoughts. (It's that human flaw known as *sinful nature*.) Imagine what life would be like if we gave up this whole idea. After all, for a group of ladies who don't want to be stereotyped or labeled, we've surely done our share of labeling others.

QUESTION: How do we fix it?

ANSWER: "'Love the Lord your God with all your heart and with all your soul and with all your mind.' This is the first and greatest commandment. And the second is like it: 'Love your neighbor as yourself.'" (Matthew 22:37–39).

Can you see them — your tiny hands and fingers as they went through the motions when you were a child? Take a moment to recall it now and yes, please do the motions. May they remind you that no matter how grand in stature or modest the structure, we the people, Christ followers, are the church; we are representatives of God's grace and love, and believe me — many are watching us.

Imagine a world where the Church Lady *mold* is shattered, where girls of every age get their identity, value, confidence, and love from a personal relationship with God, not based on the traditions of religion. Wow! Now, that's an idea! Wait . . . that's *God's* idea!

Here's another way to put it:

> *You're here to be light, bringing out the God-colors in the world. God is not a secret to be kept. We're going public with this, as public as a city on a hill. If I make you light-bearers, you don't think I am going to hide you under a bucket, do you? I'm putting you on a light stand. Now that I've put you there on a hilltop, on a light stand — shine! Keep open house; be generous with your lives. By opening up to others, you'll prompt people to open up with God, this generous Father in heaven* (Matthew 5:15–16 *The Message*).

From the first moment He thought of you, before you were born, He was madly in love with you. Our generous, loving Father created you unique, one of a kind. However, because His daughters have a kindred spirit, we — all over the world — have a lot in common. Ponder the love of the Father as you see His hand and His plan in every story of *Church Lady*.

Prayerfully the stories will resonate in your heart.
I'm Chandra Peele and I am a Church Lady — are you?

Who, Me? The Church Lady!

Again you will take up your tambourines and go out to dance with the joyful.
— JEREMIAH 31:4

erhaps you've never given this whole Church Lady idea much thought. Neither had I until one morning, I was unexpectedly awakened! Not by a loud noise or a stranger in my home, but by the gentle tugging of the Holy Spirit. He knows at 3:30 in the morning phones don't ring, kids don't call, and husbands don't need anything (most of the time, anyway). Believe me — He had my undivided attention.

In the vision I was taken to a balcony of a small, single-aisle church. As I overlooked the congregation like an old movie, everything was black and white . . . except for her. She was dressed in purple and had a tambourine in her hand. She was the only one standing up in the church while the choir was singing. She was saying, "I will praise the Lord at all times. I will constantly speak his praises. I will boast only in the Lord; let all who are helpless take heart. Come let us tell of the Lord's greatness; let us exalt his name together" (Psalm 34:1–3 NLT).

This lady — the Church Lady — was praising the Lord as freely as when King David danced naked in the street. (Please note that she wasn't naked!) I noticed the outfit she had on and the tambourine in her hand, but it was the manner in which she was praising Him — freely, with passion and joy that was so indisputable! She was uninhibited!

After I saw the woman, an arm from behind me seemed to guide my sight. I noticed others as they sat unresponsively in the pews as they, too, sang the familiar words. Some seemed distracted by the lady, others embarrassed. Resentful of the woman's freedom, others sat reserved, careful not to ruffle their religious traditions. Judgmental thoughts, though silent, could not be hidden from their faces.

As she stood in a beam of light that seemed to come down from heaven, I wondered, could her worship be so pure it was shining right into the face of God? Then I heard a whisper in my ear, *"He is the light. This lady shamelessly loves and worships the Lord! She represents the bride of Christ, the church, longing to praise and glorify her bridegroom — a beautiful example for Church Ladies everywhere!"*

Like a bird released from a cage, free to fly, this woman was free to worship. It was not the posture of her body, but the posture of her heart! Then, as though a magnifying glass were skimming the faces of other ladies in the church, I could sense a lack of joy in their hearts. Many were going through the motions, but their hearts seemed so far away (Mark 7:6). As my eyes were guided, I got a glimpse into their hearts. They were troubled, ashamed, hurt, consumed by worry and regret. Others were distracted by life — their thoughts were audible; they were all at once and mixed together. I heard some thoughts clearly: what to cook for lunch, where to go out for lunch, I chipped my toenail, and what I will wear to work tomorrow. Others were jealous, critical, and hard, certainly not joyful. The Holy Spirit was showing me the contrast of people: one free to worship while others sat restrained, and still others not really there at all. *If only they too would embrace His love and live freely in His grace.*

I think I understand, Lord, I thought. You want me to encourage ladies — Church Ladies — to praise You wholeheartedly, to freely worship You. To love! To live!

The words of David the psalmist came to me: "Those who look to you for help will be radiant with joy; no shadow of shame will darken their faces. In my desperation I prayed, and the Lord listened; he saved me from all my troubles." (Psalm 34:5–6, NLT).

Excited, a smile came over my face; I pulled my pillow close to me and closed my eyes. Then the Holy Spirit whispered, *"Yes! I want you to expose the truth! My word, My love, My power; but also to unveil the real hurts, the real needs, the real lives of my daughters, Church Ladies all over the world who are missing out on the blessings I have for them."*

My eyes widened and I sat straight up and said, "*The world?*" out loud. My words awakened my husband Bruce and he asked me if I was dreaming. "No! The Lord just gave me a vision!" Quickly I jumped out of bed to find a pen and paper, being sure not to forget a single detail. Excited and humbled that the Lord had handpicked me, an ordinary Church Lady, for such an extraordinary task, I knew He would make a way for me to share His message with His daughters — *Church Ladies all over the world!*

The next morning I shared the vision with my husband, Bruce, my daughters, and my mom, who was visiting. Although the Lord had revealed only a small glimpse of the mission, He had poured into my heart a deep desire to explore the unique characteristics of Church Ladies wherever He opened the door. And He did. The search for the Church Lady was on!

Since that night I have traveled near and far, and the Lord has opened my eyes, my mind, and my heart so that I could meet many of His marvelous daughters. She comes in many colors, shapes, and sizes. She speaks many languages, or she may just have a cute little accent of her own. She has different personalities and styles, likes and dislikes. She comes from many cultures and traditions, yet she has so much in common with other Church Ladies, her "sisters." In God's eyes she holds the title of "most beautiful," and she shines before all men! Remember the song we sang as children — "This Little Light of Mine"? Here's another way to put it:

> *You're here to be light, bringing out the God-colors in the world. God is not a secret to be kept. We're going public with this, as public as a city on a hill. If I make you light-bearers, you don't think I am going to put you under a bucket, do you? I'm putting you on a light stand. Now that I've put you there on a hilltop, on a light stand—shine! Keep an open house; be generous with your lives. By opening up to others, you'll prompt people to open up with God, this generous Father in heaven* (Matthew 5:15–16 *The Message*).

This was a huge assignment, one that I was excited to begin! Of course, I should have known that His expectations would far exceed all that I could imagine, according to Ephesians 3:20–21, which says, "Now to him who is able to do immeasurably more than all we ask or imagine, according to his power that is at work within us, to him be glory in the church and in Christ Jesus throughout all generations, forever and ever! Amen."

The Lord, however, was saying, "Wait just a minute, my precious daughter. Don't get ahead of Me. There is much for you to experience, spiritual growth that needs to take place in your own heart, before *we* share the stories."

Little did I know how much He was about to teach me. He would introduce me to Church Ladies who are full of joy, whose love for Him is pure and contagious; to those who have such a close relationship with Him that it would seem as if they sat with Him over coffee that morning. Then there would be those who were hurting, who needed healing, who needed hope. He would take me to places I had never gone to experience His love through the ministering hands and feet of Church Ladies along the journey. These experiences would change my perspective; they would broaden my mind, which would, in the end, change my heart and be a spiritual awakening.

After years of talking about this project, after meeting thousands of precious Church Ladies and collecting heartfelt stories in my journal, I began to wonder if the Lord would ever give me the opportunity to write this book. Life happens, and no matter how hard I tried to push this project to the top of the priority list, something else would always take precedence. Believe me, there were times I tried to force it and times I tried to lay it down, and as you know, a task given by God will only happen in His perfect timing.

Our heavenly Father is very creative! That's an understatement, I know. It was He that made the world and everything in it; of course He could pave the way, guide my steps, take me to both near and foreign lands *and* have me "get it" all in His perfect time. *Here's your sign!* That's exactly what happened right when I least expected it. He took off my blinders, and there right in front of me was His plan revealed. It finally all made sense. This was my destiny! Like pressing "rewind" on the video camera of my mind, snapshots begin to appear, and I began to recognize that it was God who had allowed me to stumble all those times, to slow me down so I wouldn't miss what He was teaching me. It was God who kept me from giving up on people when I went through the hurt that took me to the lowest place in the valley. When I was lonely — perhaps even depressed — it was God who watched over me, knowing the suffering would make me stronger. Looking back, I realize all those life experiences — the closed doors, the open doors, the joy, the heartache, the timely hugs, the mourning, the people passing through my life — had all been part of God's plan to prepare me for this very moment.

While on my journey in search of the Church Lady, many have crossed my path — some with stories I am certain the Lord wants me to share, while other stories are from my own experiences. As in the vision, I've witnessed Church Ladies praising Him wholeheartedly and many who have lost their joy along the way. It wasn't until recently that I saw the one in the vision I had seen years earlier, the Church Lady dressed in purple with a tambourine in her hand, joyfully praising Jesus! Tears began to flow from my eyes as if a faucet had turned on. My heart began to race, I couldn't speak, and it seemed as if the room was filled with light. There was no question — it was she! That's when I knew my search was over and that my time to share — my time to write — was *now*!

When was the last time you had a "Praise You, sweet Jesus" moment? A moment when the tears of joy were uncontrollable, your peace unexplainable, and your faith undeniable? It was a moment when you knew with everything within you that it was God! There were no other explanations! That, my sister, is when you want to dress your Sunday best, sing with all your might, and shake that tambourine (if you happen to have one) while you praise Him because you can't contain your worship.

Not only had the Lord given me the desire and inspiration to write, He has been my guide every step of the journey. Here I am, eight years after that sleepless night, writing about the Church Lady. Can you possibly know how excited I am?

God has opened my eyes. He has made it perfectly clear that if I had ever thought there was *a box* one needed to fit into to hold the title Church Lady, He did not design it. Au contraire! Instead, He has shown me that any mold we have made should be broken. His daughters are unique, beautiful, and reflect His glory most when they have been set free to be the one-of-a-kind *real* women He created them to be.

So we must reject the pigeonholes and stereotypes and agree that there is no such thing as the "perfect Church Lady." As for traditions — some are good, but others may keep us from living a life of spiritual freedom, the kind Paul talks about in Galatians 5:1: "It is for freedom that Christ has set us free. Stand firm, then, and do not let yourselves be burdened again by a yoke of slavery." Human traditions can keep us stuck in the rut of opinion; it's unfortunate that some of these age-old traditions have kept us from knowing and loving each other fully. Sister, we have so much to learn. When we believe that God loves the whole world, only then can we begin to recognize how small we are and how big He is (John 3:16). Through the pages of this book we will celebrate Church Ladies past, present, and future. If you open your heart to God's truth, there is no question — He will challenge you as you hear their stories; some from women who are very different than you, while others may be very much like you.

While you read these stories, it's my prayer that you, too, will see God in the midst of your story. When snapshots from your past come racing to the forefront of your mind, slow down, stop, take a moment to reflect, and give thanks and praise for those Church Ladies who have walked with you for a while on your journey, and for those who are in your life today. Consider their gifts, their friendship, even their differences, and for what purpose God may have them travel with you for a time. Some ladies cross our paths for a moment, some for a season, and some for a lifetime. Each one is for a specific reason (Ecclesiastes 3).

It doesn't matter about our color, nationality, wealth (or lack of it), neighborhood, the church we choose, the make and model of our car, or the brand stamped on our jeans. There are three things every woman reading this book has in common:
- God created you and loves you equally!
- You have a need for a relationship with Him.
- You were created to love the Lord God with all your heart, soul, and mind, and to love your neighbor as yourself. (Matthew 22: 37–39)

So who do you say is the Church Lady? Let me say that you might be surprised with what you discover. Take a look in the mirror. *You,* woman of God, are the *Church Lady*!

*P*RAYER

Lord, I desire to leave a lasting fragrance
of your love to everyone I meet, everywhere I go.
Make me a blessing to someone today.
Amen.

REVEAL AND TRANSFORM

I've often thought how nice it would be to have you here with me. We could chat, reminisce about all the Holy Spirit has revealed at the end of each chapter. Perhaps we can come together at a retreat or a conference, but for now I'll encourage you to let the words resonate as you read over and answer the questions for yourself. And as you do, my prayer is that the power of God will transform you by the renewing of your mind, as He has mine on this journey.

1. Has there been a time when the Holy Spirit got your attention and you knew that you knew it was God preparing you, calling you to a specific task? Did you follow through? If so, how?

2. Picture my vision. Can you see yourself in the crowd? Where are you sitting and what might you be thinking of the lady in purple with the tambourine?

3. Has reading about the thoughts of others in my vision pricked your heart? Made you think of your own thoughts and actions? Wherever and however you worship the Lord our God, next time you're there, perhaps you'll be more in tune with your mind. Write your thoughts.

4. Read Ephesians 1:22–23. Believing that we the people are the church, and *the fullness of Him who fills everything in every way . . .* what are your thoughts when considering *you* are a Church Lady?

5. Man-made traditions can keep us stuck in the rut of opinion. It's unfortunate that some of these age-old traditions have kept us from knowing and loving each other fully. When you read this statement, what were your thoughts?

CHAPTER 2

When God Winked

*See what great love the Father has lavished on us,
that we should be called the children of God!*

— 1 JOHN 3:1

When I was younger, I loved connecting the dots in coloring books. One to two, two to three, and so on. Then finally the object would take enough shape so that I could easily glide my pencil from number to number to complete the shape. Sometimes, however, I couldn't recognize the shape until the very end. Can you imagine connecting the dots blindfolded? It would be impossible! In the Christian life this is called *faith* and this, sweet sister, is a great analogy to describe my journey in search of Church Ladies around the world.

The first dot began that night of the vision. I believe the next dot was connected when I shared the vision with my family. The Lord knew I was willing and ready, but I have to admit, I never dreamed it would take eight years! With each dot, I had to wait on Him to direct me to the next dot. I knew He was at work, that the dots were connecting, but I had no clue how many remained before He would complete His beautiful piece of art. Finally, after trusting Him, enjoying the mystery, collecting stories of Church Ladies young and old, in the least suspecting place, God winked, and I knew we were on the home stretch of this amazing journey.

GOD CONNECTS PEOPLE

Within minutes of answering the phone I knew this lady was sure to be a friend for life. Although she lived in Valdosta, Georgia, and we lived in Helotes, Texas, two of God's girls made a connection that day. Putting on big events was not on Sheryl's résumé until God gave her the desire to plan a purity rally while volunteering at a teen pregnancy center. When I answered the call she said, "Hi! I'm Sheryl, and my good friend is your backdoor neighbor and she told me about your ministry."

Of course I was interested and wanted to hear more. After a good talk she asked if I would be willing to meet with her husband, Paul, who just happened to be flying over to San Antonio for a meeting the following week. Of course I agreed.

To safeguard our marriage, Bruce and I don't eat alone with the opposite sex. Wouldn't you know, Colonel Paul would be flying into an air force base within minutes of Bruce's office? I was a bit intimidated by his pilot's uniform, but Bruce (usually a man of few words) couldn't wait to talk to him about the plane he had just flown in on. Within minutes we felt like family. How wonderful that, because of Jesus, we have a kindred spirit!

From Sheryl's desire, our backdoor neighbor, the first phone call, the schools all agreeing to have me speak, the radio stations that wanted to follow us to each event, the funding, the worship band — it was evident this was a divine appointment and God was the one connecting the dots.

Then finally, after all those months of planning, two of God's daughters were entering every door the Lord had opened: every middle school and high school in Valdosta, teen pregnancy centers, lunches with Church Ladies, each joyfully doing the work our Father had called us to. The school assemblies were educational, *not* faith based. Therefore it was our hope that parents and students would attend the Pure Love conference on Saturday. At the community center, we gave the abstinence message on a biblical perspective. While teaching God's plan for marriage, the emphasis was on His love, grace, and forgiveness. The turnout was awesome! Many students gave their life to Christ and hundreds pledged to abstain from sex until marriage. We had been obedient to God's call and all the glory for a successful event was His.

The last day, Sheryl asked me to keep her family in my prayers. Although they were accustomed to frequent moves, now that Paul was a colonel, their assignment could take them anywhere in the world. She asked me to pray especially for their two sons who were in high school. Life was good for them, they were settled and involved; she was uncertain how they would react to the impending move.

GOD REVEALS THE BIGGER PICTURE

A couple of weeks later Sheryl called to tell me their new assignment was Cairo, Egypt. We prayed and asked the Lord for direction, peace, and willing hearts for her sons. Before we said goodbye, she said, "Will you come see me in Egypt?"

We laughed and I said, "Of course!" When I hung up the phone, I felt the Holy Spirit say, "*You will!*"

Fast-forward two years.

The phone rang, but the number that displayed was unfamiliar. About an hour later, the same number appeared on the caller ID. This time I answered. "Chandra! It's Sheryl!" We both did the whole girlie high-voice hello and then she said, "D you wa-a co-e to Egypt?" The crackling noise broke up her words and I couldn't understand her. Finally I realized we needed to calm down and speak slower. After all, she was calling from a landline on the other side of the world! She repeated, "Do you want to come to Egypt?"

"Sure!" I replied. "I'd love to come see you!"

"Well, you might just get your chance. God has a plan for you to come here; I just know it!" she said excitedly.

I listened with anticipation as she shared the details. They were attending the Maadi Community church just outside of Cairo when she asked the student minister if he needed help. Of course, like any good student minister, he said *absolutely*! A few weeks later Sheryl began working with a small group of expat girls and began to use *Priceless: Discovering True Love, Beauty, and Confidence*, one of my Bible studies, for a teaching tool. (I had given her a copy at the Pure Love conference.) The girls enjoyed the study and when they ordered the next book in the series, *Radiant*, the girls asked Sheryl, since she knew me, if she thought I could come over and speak to them in person. In that moment Sheryl thought, *God, You are really going to bring Chandra to Egypt!* After checking with the pastor and praying about it, the minister of youth agreed they should invite me over.

Joy was welling up in my soul as she shared these words with me! As she spoke, I listened, but at the same time I was thanking God for answering my prayer. For years Bruce and the girls have supported my ministry. They knew all those nights away from home meant Mom was doing God's work. Grateful for their understanding, I prayed specifically for the Lord to bless us with a family missions trip opportunity. Of course, now it's clear that the Lord put that desire on my heart.

I couldn't wait to tell Bruce. When I asked him if he would be interested in going, I'll never forget what he said: "Are you kidding? You're not going without me!"

"Do you think the girls could go?" I asked.

With hesitation in his voice he said, "Boy, that would be a great experience, but honey, we can't afford it. Plus, there's no way they could miss that many days of school." You know what they say — never say never!

The next day I emailed Sheryl and asked her to pray with me that God would make a way for this to be that family missions trip I had always dreamed of. I claimed 1 John 3:1: "See what great love the Father has lavished on us, that we should be called the children of God!"

I believed God's unlimited resources would make a way, and they did! My daughters were ecstatic! With ease Lindsey got permission from her professors, and our trip dates lined up with Holly's fall break. In October, one year after Sheryl's call, the Peeles were on their way to Egypt!

WELCOME TO CAIRO

After going through customs at the Cairo Airport, we gathered our luggage, and there waiting for us with smiles as big as Texas were Paul and Sheryl. I knew before we arrived that I would speak at a Sudan women's conference, but what I didn't know was that the conference began four hours after I stepped off the plane in Cairo. We were staying in their home and after they gave us a quick tour, I changed my clothes, freshened up, and we were off. Tired from the long flight and in a bit of culture shock, Bruce and the girls stayed behind while Sheryl whisked me away to speak. Now remember, Bruce had met Paul three years earlier. Amazing!

On the short drive to the church, Sheryl expressed her regret that she would need to slip out due to a prior commitment. She assured me that the pastor would get me back to her place when the event was over.

Trusting the Lord, I smiled as I remembered the words of my mission's pastor: "*Fluid* is the key word. Be ready to share your faith or serve someone the moment opportunity presents itself." I guess this was one of those moments regardless of how tired I was. Upon our arrival, the pastor was standing in the dirt driveway with a few of the women to greet us. He spoke English but most of the women did not. He introduced me to my translator, a beautiful Sudanese woman who welcomed me with a kiss on both cheeks. Then with such excitement, they showed Sheryl and me their recently finished (as in hours ago) church building. The men, maybe 30 of them, were so proud! The expressions on their faces were priceless as they walked us into the humble yet beautiful open-air church.

I could feel a migraine coming on — jet lag maybe, but most likely it was the freshly painted shellac on the beautiful wood ceiling. The pastor said, "The men (he pointed to them as they proudly nodded their heads) worked through the night to finish the project before the women's conference and your arrival today." As I raved of its beauty, the strong fumes took my breath away and I wondered how in the world I would be able to speak at all.

However, the moment the worship began (as I stood surrounded by hundreds of Sudanese women), every concern melted away. Praise was in my heart and on my lips as they sang a familiar hymn in their language: "What a friend we have in Jesus." Precious! Priceless! I'll never forget it! Even now I can hear their voices singing. As they praised our Father, they welcomed me, their friend and sister in Christ. With tears welling up in my eyes, I could barely see as I gazed around the room behind me. I knew God was with us; I felt His presence so sweet. He had planned long ago for me to be right where I was, in that exact moment.

Sheryl slipped out and there I stood in a foreign land, surrounded by people from a different culture, yet I had no fear — I was standing with my sisters. I smiled and said, "Lord, so these are Your Church Ladies in Egypt."

For the next 15 days, God (and Sheryl) had a full itinerary planned. Like all those years in Valdosta, there wasn't a moment unaccounted for until the last day. I spoke at girl schools, women's and girls' Bible study groups, the student ministry, and four services at Maadi Community Church. While I was speaking, Bruce and the girls were either with me or exploring. Of course, Bruce enjoyed spending time with Paul who came home every evening with stories to share.

From that very first night to the last, I delighted in the Lord as I observed Bruce and the girls see God at work in every detail. God was changing them and me. We felt so comfortable and incredibly welcomed by this Church Lady and her family. Every need was met and every meal taken care of. One evening a family from the church hosted a dinner for us in their home. We were shocked to find their real home is five miles from our home back in Texas (when they aren't working in Egypt). They served Texas barbecue! To think we were worried about what we might have to eat! Hospitality at its best! *Texas style* in Egypt.

Sheryl had planned day trips to see the pyramids, Old Cairo, the Egyptian museum, and of course she made arrangements for us to ride camels in the desert. My family was experiencing the kindness and hospitality of the family of God. What a life-changing experience. What a blessing!

The last thing on the itinerary was for me to speak to a group of girls. When Sheryl picked me up afterwards, she said, "That's a wrap!" and smiled as we got into her SUV. After two nonstop, power-packed weeks of ministry and excursions, our itinerary was complete. Exhausted, I leaned back into the seat. I think the instant those words entered my ears, my brain sent a message marked *urgent* to my body because it began to shut down. Then Sheryl's phone rang. The lady on the other line was the president of the Maadi Women's Guild and she was inviting me to speak at their meeting the following day. As she spoke, Sheryl mouthed her words to me. I had a momentary battle with my flesh as I thought, *Are you kidding? Seriously! God, You know how hard it is for me to say no, but I don't have the energy.* As I began to say, *No thank you,* she said, "Oh, and they are having an African Fashion Show."

Immediately Holly, who was in the backseat, spoke up. "Mom! You have to do it! We have to see the fashion show." No surprise coming from my daughter with a fashion degree.

"Well . . . OK," I said with hesitation. "How long do I . . . "

"You only have to speak for 15 to 20 minutes. (Pause.) On whatever you feel led to share. (Pause.) They would be honored to have you." She smiled as she repeated everything the woman was saying, pausing between each bit of information.

"OK," I said very unenthusiastically. "I guess I'll do it."

I closed my tired eyes and prayed, *Lord, I'm drained. I don't have anything left to give. But if this is Your will, another door You have opened, here I am. I trust You will give me the strength and the words to share.*

That night, our host planned a wonderful farewell dinner for us on the Christina, a dinner boat that cruised up and down the Nile River at sunset. It was fabulous! Seriously—can you say *lavished*? Many of our new friends joined us, and it was a very meaningful evening as we ate and celebrated what God had done. As I sat on the bow of the boat, I looked up on the deck and saw Bruce laughing and talking with the men (church men). I looked at the opposite end of the boat where Lindsey and Holly were enjoying a good conversation with college students who had come from several different states to serve in Cairo for the year. And there I was, surrounded by precious Church Ladies who had done the Father proud, I'm sure. "*Thank You, Lord, for Your special favor and for lavishing Your love on us,*" I prayed. "*Knowing we are in the place where you actually lived as a baby makes it all even sweeter. This experience has been wonderful, more than I could have asked or imagined.*"

We had a late night so I decided to get up early and spend some quiet time with the Lord. As I sat on the rooftop patio ten stories up, my Bible was opened on my lap. But my mind wandered as I gazed across the congested rooftops laced with satellite discs. I never dreamed I'd be in Egypt sharing the gospel and encouraging Christians. I never dreamed I'd be sitting on a rooftop hearing the Muslim call to prayer. But I did dream my family would go with me on a missions trip out of the country to experience God's unlimited resources. Now those dreams had come true and we would soon be leaving. With a heart filled, overflowing with gratitude, I thanked God for the friends we had made, those who had opened their homes, for the new believers, and especially for the doors He had opened—for the trip He had made possible. It was as though He had numbered the dots and we simply had to be obedient, willing to connect each one.

Wiping the tears from my eyes, I picked up my Bible and prayed, "Lord, give me the exact words You want me to share with these ladies. I don't have a clue where to begin today."

Each time I flipped the pages to a familiar passage of Scripture, He said, "No, not this one." After an hour, it was time to get dressed. Still I did not know what the Lord wanted me to share. I had peace in my heart, a confident expectation that God would give me the words. I trusted Him completely! "The Lord gives true peace to those who trust in Him alone," I whispered, as if to encourage myself.

THE MAADI WOMEN'S GUILD

A beautiful, well-put-together lady was standing at the gate of the entrance to welcome us as we arrived. She was the president, the one who had spoken with Sheryl on the phone. "We are so glad you are here, Chandra! We have heard so many wonderful things about the work you are doing and we felt the Lord might have one more thing for you to say before you leave us." As we walked inside, she told me (in her Australian accent) a little about the Maadi Women's Guild: "Although we meet at the church building and many of us are believers, this is not a church or Christian event. However, we look for every opportunity to share the love of Christ and He is always at work within our midst. Ladies come and go because Maadi is a community filled with expats from all over the world."

An expatriate (in abbreviated form, *expat*) is "a person temporarily or permanently residing in a country and culture other than that of the person's upbringing or legal residence." according to Wikipedia.

Although I had met several expat families, I hadn't paid close attention to how many lived in Maadi. The sweet lady then asked me what I'd be speaking to the women about. When I smiled and replied, "I don't really know yet," she laughed and said, "You're funny. So seriously . . . what will you speak on?" When she realized I was seriously in "waiting on God mode," she asked if she needed to get someone else to share. I assured her that I was confident the Lord would come through.

The event began and there were close to 200 women in attendance and all sitting at round tables. The girls and I were sitting up front with Sheryl, the president of the guild, and a few other attendees.

The first lady got up and welcomed everyone and then she introduced the next person in the guild, and so on. Several ladies gave reports as a prelude to the fashion show. The last woman introduced me and the girls. She said that we were visiting from the United States, and proceeded to ask everyone around the room to stand up and tell where they were from. It was a bit overwhelming when a woman on the guild announced there were 66 nations represented in the room that day. With that, she told us to sit back and enjoy the Women's Guild's first-ever African Traditional Dress Fashion Show. The music came on and the emcee told about each country as that particular model, dressed in her native attire, walked down the simple runway. Much to my surprise, the first young lady gave me a huge smile and a little wave. I recognized her as the first woman to give her life to Christ that first night I was in Egypt at the Sudan women's conference. My heart leaped! The native dresses were stunning and certainly much attention had gone into each one. The women with their dark skin flashed brilliant white smiles that seemed to shout, "I'm a believer!"

Then it happened. The last woman was dressed in purple. Her head-dress was wrapped to the side, finished with a perfectly tied bow. As she walked down the aisle, my mind instantly flashed back to that vision all those years ago. *It's her — the Church Lady in my vision!* It seemed as though the Father was saying, "Surprise!" Then He winked at me as to assure me He had this planned before He had given me the vision.

I know some people get upset when Christians say the Lord spoke to me, but sister, He did! A room full of Church Ladies witnessed it. Tears were flowing from my eyes like a faucet had been turned on. In that moment the Lord said, "Turn to Romans 12:9 and read to the end. It's time. Time to write *Church Lady!*"

My eyes were filled with uncontrollable tears of joy and I could barely read the words. Lindsey, Holly, and the president (sorry, I don't recall her name) asked me if I was OK. I think they thought I was scared to death to speak since I wasn't prepared. So funny!

What happened next was unmistakable, as if God was saying, "Daughter, I want to be sure you don't miss what I'm saying here." The lady in purple picked up a tambourine and shook it in the air as all the models formed a line and danced their way back down the aisle. I wanted to jump up and shout but instead, crying like a baby, snot and all, I simply did what God asked me to do. I read Romans 12:9–21. And as if His finger reached out of heaven and underlined each line, He gave me the written description of you — the Church Lady.

The titles of the chapters, and most of the stories, were already written; but that day He gave me the verses to connect the dots so I could finish this book. There are 13 verses from verses 9–21. There are 13 chapters remaining for you to read. Each chapter, but the last one, fits with one of these verses. God put order to my stories. He did it, not me.

Before you move on, read Romans 12:1–8 if you have a Bible handy. In chapter 12 Paul is speaking to each believer on a more personal level. He tells us to no longer conform to the world because we have been transformed, made new by faith in Jesus Christ. We should be a living sacrifice for God's purpose. When our mind is transformed, then we will know what He wants us to do. We are all parts of His body; each of us has a different job to do. And we belong to each other, so we need each other. God has given us each the ability to do certain things well. If you are a teacher, teach the best you can. If you are called to serve, serve well. If you have money, give generously. If you have the gift of kindness, do it gladly.

Girlfriend! Sister! Church Lady! Believe me when I say it's time to embrace who you are in Christ. Our lives may be different — our language, culture, the way we worship, our gifts, likes and dislikes — but it's *who* we worship that makes us a Church Lady. Our Father is calling His daughters to stand upright, to be bold, a light in this dark world; to tell others about His marvelous, merciful love! *Merciful love*, did you catch that? Not judgmental, but unconditional love! What an honor to be the daughter of the King of kings.

We may look like a mess — in fact our lives may be a mess, our families may be dysfunctional, we may be at our wits' end — but hang on, Church Lady; through it all He is preparing us for something greater. Can you say *patience*? It's taken years for Him to share each story in these pages with me so I can share them with you. I've done my part — don't miss yours! Watch and you will begin to see Him connecting the dots for His plan in your life too!

Often in our weakest moment He does His greatest work. Why? Because that is when we give Him the greatest glory! What an honor it has been to meet His daughters — Church Ladies like you — all over the *world*.

REVEAL AND TRANSFORM

Would you agree God's timing is amazing? When you look back, can you see how He has been at work in your life too? With every recollection my faith grows and now I trust Him completely!

I. Have you experienced God's plan with a first encounter, a time you knew He was at work but you couldn't put your finger on it? What was the outcome? Did you or did you not tell someone about it? Why or why not?

2. Reflecting back, was there a significant event or season where you are certain God was connecting the dots, plotting your path, moving you to complete His task for a purpose? Explain or list those that come to mind.

3. Go back and read Romans 12:1–8 again. What does Paul mean in verse 1, "to offer your bodies as a living sacrifice, holy and pleasing to God—this is your true and proper worship."?

4. In Romans 12:2, why is it so important that we no longer conform to this world? Who transforms and renews our mind? Read Romans 8:5: Because of Jesus, you and I are possessors of the Spirit and it is the H _____ S _____ who transforms our mind.

5. Do you know your self-worth? Who you are in Christ?

How are you doing in the self-worth area of your life? Where do you struggle? Confess that to the Lord; ask the Holy Spirit to renew and transform your mind in this specific area. Unfortunately, low self-esteem affects your mind, your heart, and ultimately your life.

It's freeing to know that the basis of your self-worth comes from your identity in Christ!

CHAPTER 3

My Father's Eyes

Don't just pretend to love others. Really love them.
Hate what is wrong. Hold tightly to what is good.

— ROMANS 12:9 (NLT)

Have you had any problems with your vision lately? Not too long ago I had some eye work done. In this case my doctor was the Great Physician — God, my heavenly Father. I never knew there was a problem, but He did. In an instant He made the necessary adjustments to give me *agape vision* — eyes that see with a godly love, enabling me to see others as I've never seen them before. *Could this be a glimpse of how God sees His children*, I wondered?

The Holy Spirit, my heart, and these eyes seem to work together, correcting my negative or critical thoughts. I must admit, there have been times when "I" got in the way of the "eye" God had adjusted. Thankfully, God has been merciful as He continues to show me how narrow-minded I can be. However, now that I've experienced life with agape vision, I hope never to settle for 20/20 vision again. The next time you talk to the heavenly Father, ask Him to adjust your vision. I highly recommend it!

After years of volunteering and teaching in my home church, God has given me opportunity to go public with his good news (Matthew 5:14–16 *The Message*). While my light shines for Jesus in my hometown, most of my ministry happens on the hill in other cities. These open doors have put many miles on my vehicle and I've become very familiar with airports across the country. No matter where I lay my head at night, my desire is always the same — that my light will shine bright for Jesus!

On this particular day, my bags were packed and I was on my way back home from speaking at a weekend retreat. Much to my dismay there were delays. Not too happy about this inconvenience, I found a seat at the gate and settled in for the long, boring wait. While people-watching, I spotted a group of ladies who had just treated their sweet tooth to ice cream. Talk about a fragrance! Mmm — there's just nothing quite like the smell of a warm waffle cone. Knowing I had plenty of time, I decided to indulge myself too. With two scoops of sweet-cream flavored ice cream mixed with peanut butter cups, in a chocolate-dipped waffle cone, surely my wait would seem a bit more enjoyable.

As I returned to my seat, savoring every spoonful, I went back to people-watching. After all, isn't that what you do in an airport? Besides, I was looking for the Church Lady.

"*Oh, God bless her!*" I prayed as I watched an elderly lady walk slowly down the tarmac with a sweet smile on her wrinkled face. It didn't seem to bother her that crowds buzzed by her like bees making honey. The elderly lady seemed to be moving in slow motion while everything else was in real time. *I bet she's a Church Lady,* I thought. *Patience and kindness are sure to be her gifts.*

I smiled as I licked my ice cream. That's when I saw a young mom pushing her baby in a stroller, while her toddler hung onto the hem of her dress. Watching them took me back. I couldn't help but remember Lindsey and Holly's first trip to the airport when they were about that same age. A smile came over my face and I thought, *I bet she's a Church Lady.* I could just imagine her dressing up her little girls for church — in matching dresses, no doubt — teaching them to sing "Jesus Loves Me," and tucking them into bed with bedtime prayers.

While praying a silent prayer of blessing for that mommy, my thoughts were sharply interrupted! It wasn't what I heard, it was what I saw. I did a double-take as a young woman covered in body art (to put it nicely) stopped at my gate. I couldn't help but notice others looking at her too. She had tattoos on her calves, arms, and neck. While noticing how cute her hairstyle was, I thought, *How sad! What a beautiful girl she could be without all those tattoos, poor girl.*

After a few moments, she walked over and began talking to a neatly dressed girl who had been standing across from me for quite some time.

After watching them for a few moments, I realized I was staring and quickly turned in the other direction. My daughters call it the "two-minute rule" — looking at one thing more than two minutes is considered staring, and it is not polite. They are absolutely correct.

Pretending to read the newspaper as I held it in front of my face, my ears were intently eavesdropping on their conversation. What? Did she just say "Jesus"? You know there is no other name like it, so I assumed — I just knew — that sweet young girl must be witnessing to the tattooed girl. As I prayed I asked the Lord to give her the words to speak.

"Lord, may she be open to your truth."

My prayer came to a quick halt as the lady behind the counter called for my group to board. I had lost track of time, so feeling frazzled, I quickly gathered my bags, threw away the spoon (the only thing left over from my ever-so-tasty ice cream), and got in line. Sliding my feet down the aisle with all the other passengers, my seat of choice was in sight. I like to sit on the right side of the plane one row behind the wing. You're probably thinking, *Just take a seat . . . any seat!* No, thank you, I prefer that one. The noise from the jet engines was minimal, and as I daydreamed and stared out the window, I watched the blinking light at the end of the wing. Little did I know that on this particular day there would be a reason for me to be seated in row 17, seat A.

I was tired from speaking at the retreat, so this would be a great time to rest before arriving home to my active family. Arranging my cute little floral bag under the seat in front of me and placing a blanket over my legs, I grabbed my book and opened it. I was hoping to read and get in a short nap before touching down at my final destination. It's plane etiquette — didn't you know? Anytime one is covered with a blanket and has an open book, don't interrupt!

Anyway, that's exactly when it happened. The tattoo lady I had noticed in the airport was headed straight for the seat between the bearded man seated at the end of my row and me. As she approached the aisle, she made eye contact with me. My thought was correct: not only was she taking the middle seat, which would crowd me, but she had a very large backpack that she stuffed under the seat in front of her. Then, much to my surprise, she turned to me, stuck out her hand, and with a smile that brightened her face, she said, "Hi, I'm Madison."

You won't believe what happened next. She said, "You're a believer, right?"

"Are a believer in what?" I curiously responded.

"In Jesus!" she said with a chuckle.

Somewhat in shock, I quickly responded, "Well, yes. Yes, I am."

"I knew it!" she said. "We have something to celebrate! I just shared Jesus with that girl (pointing a few rows behind us to the well-dressed blonde girl), and now we have a new sister in Christ!" Putting her hand in the air awaiting a high five, I gave it to her.

OK . . . OK . . . just imagine the look on my face. Better yet, just imagine the one on God's face. I felt terrible for what I had assumed about this girl at first glance. The Holy Spirit quickly reminded me of the message God gave Samuel: "Looks aren't everything. Don't be impressed with his looks and stature. God judges persons differently than humans do. Men [and women] look at the face; God looks into the heart" (1 Samuel 16: 7 *The Message*).

This girl, Madison, talked the entire flight. While she was talking, I was thinking, *God, You have such a great sense of humor.* You see, before getting on the flight, I shared with the Lord how I didn't want to talk to anyone on this flight, because I was too tired from ministering all weekend. No problem. He took care of that for me. God Himself sat Madison down right where He needed her to be — ministering to Chandra Peele. I sat speechless (which doesn't happen very often) as she shared her story.

Madison began telling her story before we ever left the ground. Her birth mother was a drug addict, and since age three Madison had been tossed from foster family to foster family. Although thankful for the roof over her head and a place to call home, she never seemed to fit in with the latest family of eight. Her fifth foster home was the one where something miraculous would happen. After searching for years, Madison's biological grandmother finally found her and took her home.

Before that day, Madison had been looking for love in all the wrong places. She had become good friends with a boy, whose dad was a tattoo artist. After school she would spend hours there, and unfortunately, Madison became their guinea pig — or should I say drawing board?

Clueless about her real value, this made Madison feel good — even needed, for that matter. Unaware that she was being used, she was a walking billboard for the guy's body art.

"Yeah, I got all these tattoos before I knew Jesus," she said. "It still rocks my world that, when my grandmother took me in, she was able to look past the tattoos and see the real me. Crazy, right?"

Madison shared that her grandmother never said a word about her colorful skin and body piercing; however, she requested that Madison go to church with her every Sunday. Madison had never gone to church before, so she agreed without hesitation. It wasn't long before her grandmother's love for Jesus spilled over onto her. Soon she became interested in this Jesus she had never heard of before. Then she paused for a moment, as I wondered how in the world she had never heard of Jesus before.

With a smile she said, "One by one the earrings began to come out. Although Grandmother didn't say anything about them, it seemed as if they were disrespectful or distasteful. I didn't want to hurt her, so one night I just started taking them out."

Madison gave her life to Jesus Christ, and she began to notice a change inside her.

"I remember going to bed in my very own bedroom thinking, *Is this real?*" Madison laid her forearm on the armrest between us and said, "I knew I couldn't get rid of the tattoos, but there was one here (she pointed) that really bothered me. It was a skull with a snake coming out of its mouth. It was wicked, demonic, and I hated it! Knowing this, my grandmother made a few phone calls, and before I knew it, she had an appointment for me to have it removed. During the procedure, the pain became unbearable!" Shaking her head, she described how, as she closed her eyes, trying her best not to cry out loud, it was then that the Lord spoke to her and said, "This isn't necessary, My child. My love comes without conditions. I paid your debt on the Cross. It is finished!"

"In that moment my tears of sadness and remorse turned to tears of joy!" Madison's eyes once again had tears in them as she shared her powerful story with me. She explained, "I told the guy, 'Stop!' Then I asked him if, instead of removing the skull, he could draw a new tattoo over it." She laughed out loud and said, "You should have seen the look on my grandmother's face! But I said, 'No, no, Grandmother! Not just *any* tattoo. I'd like an outline of a cross, with a banner that says, *Jesus.*'"

Wiping a tear from my eye, I touched her arm and told her it was beautiful. She went on to say that the Lord gave her a peace like she had never experienced. From that day forward, she has never felt ashamed of the ink on her body. "It's just a reminder of my past and a great setup for me to share my eternal future," she said. "I want my life to illuminate God's love so brightly that people will see past the tattoos as my life and my words point them to Jesus!"

Barely able to breathe, my heart ached as she told me how people in the church had treated her. "Now that I know about leprosy, I think sometimes that might be how they see me."

"Who are *they*?" I caringly asked.

"Church people," she answered. Lovingly she said, "I think they just automatically assume that I'm a bad girl, but it's OK. You live with your choices, and I guess this is a consequence I'll live with the rest of my life. Sometimes I wonder what people will be thinking of me when I'm eighty!" she laughed.

She then shared how the only thing that really bothered her was that after her grandmother attended that church for 22 years, the people couldn't get past her tattoos. So out of love for her granddaughter, she left her church family.

My heart was breaking, knowing I had just been one of those Church Ladies who stamped her with "DEFECT" before ever giving her a chance. I was so ashamed. *Oh Lord, forgive me for judging this precious child of Yours*, I silently prayed as she continued.

Another time, several ladies in her youth group pulled her aside and told her that she would need to wear clothes that concealed her tattoos when she came to church, even at summer camp. I wanted to hug her tight and apologize for all the Christians in the universe who had hurt her. Unfortunately, I knew that would include me.

Only God could have shielded Madison's tender heart from the actions and words of "church people." Miraculously, it seemed none of the hurt had taken root in her heart.

Madison had a burning desire to share her story of being lost and then found (literally) to anyone who would listen. "I am so thankful to God!" she said. "Each time I share my story, it's like thanking Him over and over again. God loves me unconditionally, and His love and grace is really the only thing worth sharing, right?" she asked.

Amazingly, she didn't let the stares and the whispers hurt her, not even those from Church Ladies like me. She held her head high, knowing that His grace had set her free. Through an intimate relationship with Jesus Christ, the Word of God, and the Holy Spirit's power, she gained a new confidence. She made herself available, and the Lord said, "Come, follow me."

This girl lives with purpose! I thought. Jesus calls each of us who believe that He is the Son of God, the Savior of the World, to proclaim the good news! "'Come, follow me,' Jesus said, 'and I will send you out to fish for people.'" (Matthew 4:19).

At age 21, Madison travels the United States and abroad, sharing the gospel story of Jesus Christ, as He directed: "Go into all the world and preach the gospel to all creation. Whoever believes and is baptized will be saved, but whoever does not believe will be condemned" (Mark 16:15–16).

Wow! Have you ever judged a person and found out later you were *so* wrong? Funny when we see things from a different perspective how quickly our opinion can change.

This young Church Lady blessed me! Not only did she minister to me, her story greatly impacted my life. God used her to change my heart. Meeting Madison gave me a fresh perspective while looking for the Church Lady. There is no specific race, color, shape, dress, size, fancy hat, Bible size, or hairstyle that makes us a Christian (a Church Lady). Each child of God is unique. Body and soul, she is marvelously made! (Psalm 139:14 *The Message*)

Talk about a wake-up call! It is clear to me the Lord needed to adjust my eyesight before I continued on my journey in search of the Church Lady. Madison had been transformed from the inside out. The Lord needed to show me that Church Ladies look like Him on the inside, regardless of what they look like *to me* on the outside.

Madison sat in row 17, seat B, not by accident, but as a divine inter-vention. God used Madison to teach me more about His unconditional love and to uncover and shine light on my judgmental ways. For much too long, my vision has been blurred by the world's view of what the Church Lady looks like. Unfortunately, I was unaware that I, too, had stereotyped people. How merciful of the Lord to use Madison to validate my purpose in ministering to Church Ladies. It's a big responsibility and one not to be taken lightly! We Church Ladies can all learn from Madison.

Oh Lord, please help me, I prayed. *Forgive me for being so quick to make assump-tions of others; forgive me for my self-righteous ways. Thank You for reminding me of Your beauty found in those who surround me. Open my eyes so that I can see others as You see them. Amen.*

THE REAL PROBLEM

How simple-minded of me to think that all Church Ladies were raised in church, much less the church in which I had grown up. While wanting to break the stereotype for the Church Lady, I had created a stereotype of my own (Church Ladies don't have tattoos). Please, who am I to think I could pick her out by the way she looks or how she is dressed? The elderly lady in the airport, the young mommy with the two children — how could I have so quickly made the assumption that they were both Church Ladies? Could it be that I have assumed far too often, and because of my prejudgments, have passed by opportunities to tell others about God and His great love for them? Who am I to assume that, just because the young girl across from me had a certain look, that she knew Jesus?

I'm ashamed for my actions. However, sharing my shortcomings and un-Christlike behavior may be just what the doctor (the Lord) uses to adjust *your* eyesight too. I'm thankful for Madison, who boldly shares her story and God's amazing love with everyone, even Church Ladies like me.

During my life as a Christian, I have seen some incredible God-sized changes made when testimonies of truth are shared. Truth exposes us, strips away any façade we stand behind. There's just something liberating that happens when we quit trying to prove ourselves and admit that, just like the next person, we have or have had issues. We're going to mess up. Praise the Lord — He will continue to pick us up. What great joy we have knowing God will help us in the midst of our wayward human acts! Our heavenly Father pulls us out of the miry muck of this world, just like He did Madison. He lovingly and mercifully dusts us off and gets us headed in the right direction again. Life isn't like a DVR. We can't speed through life's yucky parts, but we can trust that God will help us persevere.

> *Let perseverance finish its work so that you may be mature and complete, not lacking anything. . . Blessed is the man who perseveres under trial because, having stood the test, [he] will receive the crown of life that [God] has promised to those who love him* (James 1:4, 12).

Thank You, God, for using Madison's story of perseverance to help me see others with agape eyes.

My beautiful sister, God knows your heart. He has walked and talked with you. He knows your desire to reflect Him in all that you do and say. So how can you see others through His eyes? The answer: you need your vision changed. After meeting Madison, there is no question that I needed the Lord to improve my vision, not just because I'm over 40 and no longer have 20/20 vision — no, that's not the kind of vision I mean. We need to have *agape vision*. Beginning to see others with agape eyes, with

His love, gives me a glimpse of how He looks at the world, how He looks at me, and how He looks at you.

So, who is the Church Lady? From those who lived centuries ago, to the modern Christian women of today, there's only one that gives us the privilege to be called a Church Lady, and His name is Jesus. Do we look different? Oh yes, indeed. Hairstyles, clothing trends, shoe design, culture, all of it is ever changing, but there is One who always stays the same — *Jesus!*

The Church Lady loves the Lord. She worships and praises Him. She serves Him. She seeks His wisdom in every circumstance. She passionately lives her life to bring glory to Him. Her love for God is obvious! Does she make mistakes? Yes. But she trusts God to teach her, to mold her, and shape her as she so desperately desires to reflect Him more.

EYES LIKE YOURS

Today, as I lie under this old oak tree (must be over 100 years old), I can't help but keep my eyes on all that surrounds me in this big open space. These huge branches hang to the ground, resembling an umbrella. I see bright blue sky peeking through the leaves and bare branches.

Then my focus comes closer as I notice the tiny red ladybug crawling on a bright green leaf. I can't help but see God's hand in it all, as I know heaven is above that which I can see.

My glance keeps coming back to the branches of this big old tree. It's huge! The carving in the trunk, the ants crawling in a straight line, heading for a hole so tiny but oh-so deep. The moss that clings to every other branch is so beautiful and created by the One who created me. Then, lying so still, trying my best to not so much as blink, my eyes stare as they watch two redbirds on the branch just above my head. The color red is brilliant as it rests against the green leaf.

As I listen to their song, the beautiful music that comes from these tiny little birds, a gentle breeze blows against my face. It's as though I feel the breath of God in the stillness of this divine moment. Wait. I think my vision is becoming clearer. Could this be how God himself looks at His creation — a bird's eye view of every single living thing? Is this what I miss every day — the simple things? His beauty? His creation?

In this moment, my prayer became a humble cry. Wiping the tear that had rolled down the side of my face, I prayed, "Oh God, that I could be still more often, that I might take the time to see Your creation more often, that my eyes would be opened to see people as I see Your beauty in the creation You have placed all around me. Change my heart through my eyes, Lord. Help me to see as You see."

Leaving the ranch, getting back to my normal surroundings, the Lord began to answer my prayer — I couldn't take my eyes off of people. They were fascinating! Every move, every statement, every cry from a baby, each responsive act caught my glance and turned my watchful stare into an appreciating gaze. In that moment, my eyes were off me, and my focus was on others. Today, more than any other day, I felt I could really love others with a genuine love. I could see into the hearts of the people around me. At the grocery store, at the mall, the lady behind the counter, the beggar on the street corner, the little girl who rides her bike down the block, the neighbor pulling weeds from her garden. Could it be that this is just a glimpse of the unconditional love God has for me? I wonder how many of these people, who so desperately need love, may have never experienced the sweet love of God. With these new eyes, this new vision, I have a fresh desire to show people *that* love.

God gave me more than human vision, He gave me agape vision. From the beggar on the street corner with dark teeth and dirty clothes, to the new employee nervously messing up behind the counter, to the seemingly perfect high school girl walking past me looking great but staring through the crowd with empty eyes, the widow who is lonely, the sick who need healing, the poor who need a helping hand, the child who needs to be heard — God loves them all!

Excited, I wondered what it would be like to step out into the world each day with eyes wide open, ready to see what God, the Creator, has set into motion. I would love more. I would laugh more. I would serve more. I would rest more. I would give more. I would glorify God more!

*P*RAYER

Oh Lord, that You would continue to adjust my human vision. That in each moment You would give me grace to see, a heart that's open, and a joy that not only brings new light to my eyes but that spreads like fire to those around me. Oh Lord, give me Your eyes — agape eyes.

REVEAL AND TRANSFORM

1. Before reading this chapter did you think your spiritual eyesight was in pretty good shape? After hearing Madison's story do you need a spiritual eye adjustment?

2. Looking back, would you agree you too make *Unintentionally Presumptuous Assumptions?* That's a mouthful, I know but . . . prayerfully large and in charge, they will keep me from misjudging the character of others as I did with Madison. Now when my mind sways toward this ungodly action, I simply remember UPA. Perhaps it will come in handy for you too.

3. One of the greatest lessons learned in search of the Church Lady is that God doesn't look at the outer appearance that includes tattoos (bad choices) from the past. He looks at the heart of you, me, the lady next door, and the ladies around the world. Loving others with a genuine love and displaying the attribute of agape vision (agape love) can change the world. What has the Holy Spirit revealed to you from Madison's story? Are you being transformed?

4. If you shared Romans 12:9 with someone today, what analogy might you give?

5. Is there a specific area where you need an eye adjustment from the Great Physician today?

The Nose Ring

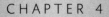

Love each other with genuine affection.

— ROMANS 12:10 (NLT)

A woman who is beautiful but lacks discretion is like a gold ring in a pig's snout (Proverbs 11:22). These were the first words that came to mind the day I heard my daughter Lindsey had gotten a nose ring. Can you imagine? There I was, miles from home, minutes from speaking at a state girls conference with the theme none other than, Godly and Beautiful. "Please, God. Tell me this isn't true!" I prayed. As feelings of anxiety suddenly plagued me I couldn't help but wonder, "What in the world will people think of me if my *own daughter* has a nose ring? Will my ministry to teens come to an end?" To say the least I was in a tizzy!

In the Peele home we don't keep secrets — maybe because we're just so bad at it. That's what happened the day I got the phone call. Holly knew her sister — who was a freshman in college at the time, had gotten her nose pierced — and she couldn't wait for me to find out.

She called and asked, "Have you talked to Lindsey today?"

"No, I haven't. Why?"

"Nothing." She responded with a giggle in her voice.

Don't you just hate that? "What do you mean *nothing*? Is everything OK? What did she do?" I asked.

"Well, why don't you call her and ask her what she did last night? But don't tell her that I told you to ask her. I'll give you a hint: nose."

Like I said, it's hard for us Peele girls to keep secrets.

Literally 20 minutes from speaking at the conference, I couldn't stand the suspense. I called Lindsey a few minutes after Holly hung up.

"Hi, Lindsey. How's my sweet girl today?" I said.

"I'm good! How are you doing? How's the conference going?" she asked.

"Oh, Lindsey, the Lord is really at work here. The worship last night was awesome and I can hardly wait for tonight! What did you do last night?" I asked.

"Nothing really, hung out with my friends, did some homework, you know?" she said.

"OK. I just wanted to make sure you were OK. I had you on my mind a lot today," I said.

"Well . . ." she sighed.

"I'm sorry, did you say something?" She hadn't but it sounded like she wanted to.

"Umm . . . nope," she mumbled.

"OK. Well you have a great day. I'm praying for you. Wish you were here. Love you. Good night." I ended the call.

The suspense was grueling. Had Lindsey gotten a nose ring, or did one of her roommates get one? I could sense the struggle in her voice. Mother's intuition, I'm sure. I prayed, "Lord, I'm not with Lindsey, but You are. Keep her safe and close to You. Whatever she has done let me stay calm so I can share your Truth with these girls here tonight. Lindsey knows she can tell me anything and that I'll always love her no matter what. Lord, don't let her sleep tonight without telling me what she is hiding. Amen."

God was merciful and used me in spite of myself. After the conference I went to my room and I had a message from Lindsey: "Call me." So I did.

"Lindsey, you wanted me to call?"

"Yes, ma'am. I need to tell you something, Mom," she said with nervous laughter.

"What is it, honey?" I asked

"Mom, don't freak out, but I did something that I know you aren't going to be happy about."

Oh my goodness! I thought. Everything imaginable ran through my mind as a knot the size of Pikes Peak wailed up in my stomach. Trying my best not to overreact, I swallowed and asked, "Lindsey, what is it?" I really wanted to ask, "*Lindsey Nicole! What in the world have you done?*" But I knew that wasn't the approach I should take.

"Well, Mom, it's not that big of a deal." She was trying to downplay it, I was sure.

"I got my nose pierced."

"I'm sorry, honey. What did you say?" I asked intently, like a person who is hard of hearing.

"Mom, I said I got my nose pierced. Everyone is doing it. It's not that big of a deal. You can hardly see it!" she explained.

Immediately I had a picture of a pig with a gold ring in its snout. I couldn't help but think what people would think of her, and worse — of me!

For a few moments I had forgotten that I get my worth from God, who loves both me and my daughter unconditionally, not from what others think. Pictures of her face with a nose ring hanging from her nose were flashing though my mind like a neon sign in Time Square. I took a deep breath in and breathed out slowly before I responded. Still my tongue spewed exactly what was on my mind. There was no containing it!

"Lindsey. Next weekend is the family reunion. What will your grandmother and your great-grandmother and all my aunts think about you? I don't know. Maybe you shouldn't go," I said.

"Mom, that's crazy. Are you serious? I can't believe you are saying that." There was disappointment in her voice.

"Lindsey, here I am speaking to girls about true beauty. How can God use me to minister to students if I can't keep my own children out of trouble? What will people think when they see that my daughter has a nose ring?" As you can sense, I lost my calm and I was way out of control. You have to understand, too, that I hadn't known anyone with a nose ring at that time — my daughter was the first.

"Mom, it's not a nose ring, it's a tiny cute little diamond earring on one side of my nose. You can barely see it! I'm going to let you go now before you or I say something that we shouldn't. I'm sorry that you are so disappointed in me." Crying, she said, "Bye!"

And with that, there was a click on the line.

Immediately I called Bruce. The first thing he said was, "No way!" And like me he asked, "What will our friends and family think, not just about Lindsey but about us?" Had she gotten mixed up with the wrong crowd? You can imagine the questions running through our minds, not to mention the shame. I was raised to believe that good Christian girls don't get anything pierced but their ears. (FYI: I've never found that in the Bible.)

The next morning while sitting at the gate at the Denver airport, I called Lindsey. There was no answer. I called again and again and finally she answered the phone. "What, Mom? You mean you are actually going to talk to someone who has her nose pierced?" I had hurt her and now she was hurting me back. If you have a daughter or you are a daughter (and you are), you know what I mean.

"Mom, I don't understand something. You have always taught me to be myself and to love the person God created me to be. I'm not a bad girl, and I would never purposely disappoint you and Dad. I just think it's cute, so I did it. I'm sorry if this one choice has *ruined* my character and yours. And Mom, you always say that Jesus looks at the heart. If my own family wants to judge me in a negative way just because I have a tiny little fake diamond on the side of my nose, that's not very godly of them. And if you are embarrassed of me and think I have *ruined* your ministry, then I guess you are a hypocrite. You've taught me that our security comes from the Lord. If that is true, how could something I do ruin the ministry that God has given you? Like you always say, God loves me and He knows my heart. I don't think God is embarrassed of me because I got my nose pierced. Beauty comes from within, remember?"

Wow! I realized she really had listened to what we had taught her all these years. She was acting very mature, and at this moment, she was teaching me.

"You're right, Lindsey. I'm sorry that I overreacted. Forgive me for making such a big deal about such a small thing. You have been such a blessing to your dad and me. We're so proud of you. *But I still can't believe you got your nose pierced!*" We laughed.

While we shouldn't judge parents based on what their children do, it happens. Even Church Ladies make accusations based on what the children of others do. Think about it: we started this bad habit when our children were still in diapers. Funny, but if a child was a biter, we looked at the parent as if they bit our child.

That next weekend Lindsey came home and I was pretty ashamed of myself after I saw the piercing. It was nothing like I had imagined. She went to the family reunion and although a few comments were made regarding the glitter on her nose, I stood humbled by her side and held my head high. Do you know by her sophomore year the tiny stud was gone, the hole was closed? And you can't tell anything was ever there.

Soon after this ordeal, I was speaking at a missions conference, and a missionary from India was sharing her testimony. You guessed it: she had a diamond on the side of her nose and she was radiant with the love of Christ. God continues to teach me every day that when He says He looks at the heart, that is truly what He means. How spiritually immature of me to one, freak out that my daughter got her nose pierced; and two, to be so concerned about what others might think. Every time I see a sparkle on a girl's nose, I smile and whisper a prayer, *"Oh Lord, thank You for your constant chiseling of my heart."*

OUR CHILDREN ARE GOD'S FIRST

God blessed Bruce and me with two beautiful daughters. One of the hardest lessons for me to learn: they are not a mint me. Nope, not God's plan at all! God created them in His image with a unique spirit, personality, likes/dislikes, spiritual gifts and talents. After years of hoping they would be leaders in youth group, be on dance team, speak up when they spoke, the president of student counsel, or at least be in student counsel, it just wasn't going to happen. It isn't their stubborn will (like I had assumed many times), it was mine. After all, the Father desires for His children to reflect Him, not their mom. When I finally realized this, life got easier for everyone. My prayer for Lindsey and Holly became, "Not my will, but Yours, Lord!" Besides, there is no greater joy than to see your children reflect the character of Jesus Christ.

The mother-daughter relationship is one of the most challenging of all times. Would you agree? First, we are Mommy: loving, teaching, feeding, putting bandages on boo-boos, knowing a kiss or a back rub made it all better. We read bedtime stories and say prayers every night just before tucking them in, snug as a bug. Then somewhere between sixth and eighth grade, we actually embarrass them by just showing up. Once she enters high school we don't really know anything — that's "in vogue," anyway. But she, on the other hand, knows everything! And out of nowhere during junior and senior year, Mommy has become Mom or Mother. The tone of her voice and her attitude toward her mom can be hurtful. Then there's shopping: the crying in the dressing room just because you are looking at her, the disbelief in her face when you explain you don't have $100 to spend on a pair of trendy jeans. It's hard to know where to look or what to say because it seems that whatever we do is wrong.

Then in the blink of an eye she turns back into her sweet self when she wants or needs something. And whatever you do, DON'T befriend her friends! But DO be quick to drop everything you are doing to tend to her every need. Daughters wants us to be "the cool mom," but not too cool. They want their friends to like us, but not too much. They want us to dress trendy, but not better than they do. Then somewhere by the end of college you enter . . . *the twilight zone.* You think you're her friend but she still needs her mom. She requests her independence, yet she is still dependent on you to answer every text or call day or night. She wants your opinion before she makes a decision on her future; but be careful, don't act like anything is your idea. This is a good place on the board game of life.

The next step — independence. Whether graduating from college or moving away from home, they look at us to see what we're thinking but they really don't want us to say anything at all. If you can understand that, you've been where I've been.

During this chapter of life, I'm walking a fine line: teaching when needed, giving wisdom when asked, and listening every time they need to talk. We laugh together, cry together, yell and scream (thankfully not very often), then laugh some more, and start all over again the next day. We support each other in the good times and the bad. I guess you could say I'm experiencing a sweet spot, also known as the "cherished mom and friend" season of life. Love each other? Unconditionally! Not for a moment or a season but for a lifetime. Even longer! Knowing we are sisters in Christ gives us the hope of eternity, a home in heaven where we will live together forever.

You know the best thing about genuine love is that it has no conditions.

NOT **MY** DAUGHTER

Holly, our youngest, was accepted into the school of her dreams the January before she graduated from high school — the Fashion Institute of

Design and Merchandising in Los Angeles, California. And it's a long way from home! Holly is the daughter who always came home before midnight, even though it was a sleepover; the one who got homesick after only three days at summer camp. We couldn't help but wonder how she would make it for two years of college, but her drive and determination said she was ready.

Like most parents, the day we left her standing in the parking lot of her college apartment, we waved good-bye as long as we could. With the tears streaming down my face, I could see the anxious but excited smile on hers. God had given us peace like only He can, but I still cried for hours as we began the 1,200-mile journey back home. In the days and weeks that followed, Bruce may have thought I was losing my mind, if not for the stories we had heard from friends who had already released their child from the nest. Some days I couldn't control my emotions no matter how hard I tried. One day as I lay on her bed, I said out loud, "God, why does this bird-flying-out-of-the-nest thing hurt so much?" And then I cried hard, like a kid with crocodile tears and snot dripping from my nose. Some days I felt sadness, others excitement, and others fear. Then before I knew it she had been in LA for a while. After a year of bumps in the road, the road always seemed to smooth out rather quickly. College was great, classes were challenging, grades were good; however, the roommate situation, the living away from home, the loneliness of this 20-year-old girl was getting the best of her, and more than we knew.

This particular semester she was living with a girl who was from the area and who had a serious boyfriend. Therefore the roommate was rarely at home, which left Holly home alone more often than not. This wasn't what she had in mind when she dreamed of the college life in sunny California, but she wanted us to think she was handling it all just fine.

One night at 11:30, alone in her apartment, she got a phone call. It was Dad (Bruce) calling to tell her that Lindsey had been in a car accident and was in ICU. He assured her that Lindsey was going to be OK and that we would keep her current with any news. Holly wanted to take the next flight home, but Dad thought it would be best for her to stay at school. Besides, Lindsey was in good hands and her injuries weren't life-threatening. Holly desperately wanted to be with us, but she understood. However, the dark cloud that had been hovering over her (unforeseen to us) was now pressing her down into a spiraling black hole. She tried to focus on her schoolwork, but Lindsey's condition and going home consumed her thoughts.

Back home, not only had Lindsey been in a serious car accident and in ICU, we were moving to Houston in ten days. In fact the day we brought Lindsey home, the packers were waiting for us at the front door.

With the trauma to her head and seven broken ribs, Lindsey couldn't be left alone. Friends (Church Ladies) came and took care of Lindsey upstairs while I was busy taking and making phone calls and answering questions from the ladies who were putting everything we owned into boxes. That week was a blur, but as scheduled, ten days after Lindsey's wreck, we made a bed in the back of my SUV and off we went to our new home.

On the way, Holly called and begged to come home. I could hear anguish in her voice, so I told her if she could get a flight home, to take it. Her flight got in at midnight and it was great to have the four of us together the first night in our new home.

Holly was a huge help. She stayed by Lindsey's side while I unpacked all those boxes. Four days later, it was time for her to go back to LA. Although it had been a short visit, she felt better after being at home and spending some time with her sister.

Holly seemed different, though — more reserved, thinner. There was a check in my spirit; something wasn't right with my sweet girl. When I asked her about it, she said she could handle it: "It's just a little homesick thing, I guess. I'll get over it." Still, I wasn't completely sold on her response. With tears in her eyes, I dropped her off at the airport, knowing it would be a few months before we would see her again.

Six weeks later, Lindsey was much better. Since Holly was still missing home, trying her best to stick it out until her next break, it seemed like the perfect time for Lindsey to go for a visit. Besides, who in Houston doesn't want to escape the heat to enjoy the sunny 70-degree weather in California?

Lindsey called to give us a safe arrival call but also expressed real concern for her sister. "Mom, Holly is not OK. She is very thin, can't eat, and cries every time she talks. I think she needs to come home."

Concerned, I shared this with Bruce and his response was, "No. We just need to go visit her and get her through this homesickness. She'll be OK."

So after Lindsey came back home, Bruce and I went out to see Holly three weeks later. When I saw her at the airport, I immediately knew it was time for us to do something to help her, even if that meant coming home for a quarter. Bruce was in denial; he was determined that our visit would make it all better. He called the school and made an appointment with the counselor. At the meeting, the counselor raved about Holly's work. She shared that Holly was a dream student on the FIDM campus and that she would have many opportunities to be placed in a great job after graduation. She encouraged Holly and said she had never seen anyone get so close and quit. As she spoke, Holly sat in her chair and was kind but passive.

After the meeting, Bruce put his arm around Holly as we walked to the car. I could tell that he was optimistic. He thought for sure those positive words would change Holly's mind, but I knew it wasn't about finishing school. There was something more going on with Holly.

Once we got to the car, Bruce said, "Wow, Holly! You are doing awesome, sweetie! We are so proud of you. Three more months and you'll be finished!"

Holly said nothing.

"Holly," Bruce said, "after all of that, all those encouraging words, are you saying that you still want to give up and go home?"

Holly began to cry. Being a pleaser, she didn't want to let her dad down. That was what had kept her there for the past three months. When we got back to her apartment, we sat in silence for at least ten minutes. Then she said, "Dad, do you hear that clock, tick-tock, tick-tock?"

"Now that you brought it to my attention, yes I do," he said calmly.

She said, "That is the only noise I have been able to hear for months now. I hate that stupid clock!"

Immediately Dad went over and took the clock off the wall and removed the batteries from it. "There," he said, "the ticking has stopped!"

Within minutes Bruce was on the phone renting a U-Haul truck. The very next day, we were driving Holly back home to Houston.

After counseling with our doctor, she said that Holly was experiencing circumstantial depression. There had been so many circumstances that had happened all at once, that Holly could not handle them. I wondered how this could happen to *our* daughter. The doctor answered my question:

• Moving every three months to a new apartment with new roommates.
• Moving in with a roommate that was never home.

- Loneliness.
- New school. New city. New people. New teachers.
- Sister was in an accident.
- Wasn't able to say good-bye to the home which she had known.
- Moved to a new home.
- All this combined made her feel that nothing was stable in her life.

"That's a lot of change for anybody," she said.

She prescribed some medicine for Holly that should help, and after several weeks of getting it in her system, finally we were getting our Holly back.

I never dreamed that my daughter, who was happy, healthy, loved, provided for, at the school of her dreams, and who has a relationship with Jesus Christ would ever become depressed. Never say never, Church Lady! We are not removed from the struggles of this world (John 16:33b; Colossians 2:1). But we can trust that the Lord will walk with us through the storm.

When we see a change in our children, we need to address it and help them through it. Although I have heard some religious people say that you don't need to see a doctor or take medication for depression, I believe that God gives doctors the knowledge to heal. Bruce and I were willing and ready to do whatever it took to make Holly better. Yes, we were praying for wisdom, and we believe in the power of prayer. We are thankful that our doctor knew what medication she needed to make her well again.

A PARENT'S RESPONSIBILITY

Moses shared what the Lord had told him to teach the Israelites before they entered into the Promised Land:

> "And you must love the Lord your God with all your heart, all your soul, and all your strength. And you must commit yourselves wholeheartedly to these commands I am giving you today. Repeat them again and again to your children. Talk about them when you are at home and when you are on the road, when you are going to bed and when you are getting up" (Deuteronomy 6:5–7).

When our children were born, we dedicated them to the Lord. We made a commitment to love them, to care for them, and to teach them to fear the Lord and to obey Him. Why? Because God promises that when we do, both we and our children will be blessed.

When I see Lindsey or Holly mess up, I feel responsible for her, but not for her actions, both positive and negative. With the nose ring, my first thought was, *Oh no! What will people think of me because of my daughter's actions?* In Holly's case, when she became depressed, she didn't want to tell me because she thought that I would be disappointed in her. When we experience freedom in Christ, we don't worry about what others think, but instead what God thinks.

Although circumstances may bring us into a stormy season, it doesn't mean it will end in disaster — God's timing is astounding and His power and provision trustworthy. Our parents could not shield us from the storms of life, nor can we protect our children from every wrong choice and broken heart. Instead we see the growth and watch them bloom into beautiful, responsible people.

As inevitable as the spring rain, the storms of this life will come. Praise the Lord for His promise of the newness of life that sprouts after the storms. Mistakes in this life shape us when we allow them to; we find out who we are, and who we are not. From one Church Lady to another: remember, our purpose is to love our children unconditionally, to teach them the Bible, God's Holy Word, and to live life as an example.

REVEAL AND TRANSFORM

When Lindsey or Holly mess up, I feel responsible for her, but not for her actions, both positive and negative. With the nose ring, my first thought was, *Oh no! What will people think of me because of my daughter's actions?* In Holly's case, her thought was, *Oh no! What will Mom think if she knows I'm depressed?* We ladies sure heap unnecessary coals on our own heads, don't we? Oh the joy that comes when we experience freedom in Christ — we don't worry about what others think, but instead what God thinks. Say this out loud: My Father loves me with all my flaws.

When the girls were in elementary and middle school, a group of ladies met at a friend's house every Tuesday and we prayed Scripture for our children. We prayed Psalm 51:10–12 for our daughters many times

through years: "Create in [her] a pure heart, Oh God, and renew a stead-
fast spirit within [her]. Do not cast [her] from your presence or take your
Holy Spirit from [her]. Restore to [her] the joy of your salvation and
grant [her] a willing spirit, to sustain [her]." Today, my girls are out of
college and I continue to pray this Scripture for them.

1. When you pray for your children, use God's Word and make it personal by adding their names. Is there a particular verse you like to
   pray? Write it here and take a moment to pray Scripture for your
   children, your spouse, your parents, and yourself right now.

2. One thing each story had in common was the first reaction: shame!
   What will my church friends think of me now? Church Lady, we — you and
   me — are real people. God wrote the Bible, and guess *who* the char-
   acters are: people like you and me, people with real hurts and needs.
   This life is not easy! Have you experienced shame, embarrassment,
   or hurtful reactions concerning your children or someone in your
   family? How did this affect you?

3. Now, shoe on the other foot: have your critical comments caused
   someone shame? The Golden Rule — do unto others as you would
   have them do to you — applies here. Consider you might be the one
   needing forgiveness before the day is over.

4. Your security doesn't come from who and what your children do, but
   who you are in Christ. What are your thoughts when you consider
   the unconditional love the grandmother had for Madison? What a
   beautiful example!

5. *"And you must love the Lord your God with all your heart, all your soul, and all your*
   strength. And you must commit yourselves wholeheartedly to these commands I am
   giving you today. Repeat them again and again to your children. Talk about them
   when you are at home and when you are on the road, when you are going to bed and
   when you are getting up" (Deuteronomy 6:5–7).

It is our obligation to teach our children the Word of God. They may disappoint us; they may humiliate us and cause us grief, but regardless they are our children and we love them with a genuine love. We can give our children everything under the sun, all the material possessions they desire, but the Word of God hidden in their heart is the most valuable gift we can give them: "Start children off on the way they should go, and even when they are old they will not turn from it." (Proverbs 22:6).

6. If you have a wayward child, read Luke 15:11–31 and be encouraged!

I'm so thankful that God blessed me with two daughters, and there are many reasons why. One, so that I could speak from experience to encourage other moms. Two, so I can be a voice for moms to daughters. If you're a mom, you can imagine the stories I hear in the midst of girls' ministry. The mother-daughter relationship is the most challenging relationship of all times. We laugh together, cry together, yell and scream, then laugh some more, and start all over the next day. We hold each other up for support in times of weakness, like the trellis of a tomato vine. On the other hand we let each other down, like having a chair pulled right out from under you unexpectedly! Love each other? It's called unconditional love, not just for a moment, or a season, but for a lifetime. The best thing about genuine love is that it has no conditions.

LETTING GO

It's hard letting go. When Lindsey and Holly went to college, I cried like a baby. I didn't go into Lindsey's room until two weeks after she had been gone. And when I did, I lay on her bed holding her teddy bear and cried like a baby. Of course I never dreamed in that moment she would have her nose pierced, but I did pray that I could let her go.

Bruce and I had always prayed that our children would have that solid foundation before they graduated from high school so they would be spiritually prepared to stand on their own two feet when they went into the real world. Now it seemed the Lord was holding me to those prayers. Very quickly I found that it is one thing to say you have let them go and another to really do it. It's a huge test of trust, trusting in the Lord to watch over them when we cannot.

I prayed specifically for Lindsey during her freshman year in college, Psalm 37:23–24: "The Lord makes firm the steps of the one who delights in him; though he may stumble, he will not fall, for the Lord upholds him with His hand."

Believing that parents are called and empowered by God — and knowing that God promises, "If [any parent] lacks wisdom, ask God [. . .] and it will be given to them" (James 1:5) — I couldn't help but wonder where I had gone wrong. After years of student ministry, I had counseled many parents when their teen messed up, or they, the parents, were at their wits' end. But this was the day I realized never say never.

CHAPTER 5

Mrs. Church Lady

And take delight in honoring each other.

— ROMANS 12:10 (NLT)

*I*f the age-old saying "give and you will receive" is true, then perhaps this verse in Romans 12 is one Christian wives should give some attention to. With 50 percent of all marriages ending in divorce for reasons such as lack of communication, loss of interest, and lack of sexual gratification, I think this subject is worthy of some "talk time."

Whether you're still writing thank-you notes for wedding gifts, or you're an empty nester, or you're somewhere in between, wouldn't you agree that every married woman hopes for a kind, loving, attentive, and giving husband, one who honors her?

In Ephesians 5:22, Paul teaches that wives should submit to the leadership of her husband. Unfortunately some have the wrong idea when they hear the word *submission* and they disregard the teaching of this very important verse. Let me clarify the meaning. To *submit* means to honor, and is very different than *to obey*. To obey means to do as one is told. To honor means to serve out of love and respect. Paul is clearly referring to a spiritual leader who serves his wife just as Christ served His disciples. It's truly a beautiful picture of honor and an example we should follow to assure a happy and healthy marriage. Can you imagine if more husbands and wives honored one another?

The instructions for a happy and healthy marriage are:
• Husband loves and honors God.
• Husband loves and honors his wife.
• Wife honors God.
• Wife honors her husband.

A wife who honors Christ should also honor her husband. Paul teaches,

> *"For this reason a man will leave his father and mother and be united to his wife, and the two will become one flesh. This is a profound mystery — but I am talking about Christ and the church. However, each one of you also must love his wife as he loves himself, and the wife must respect her husband"*
> (Ephesians 5:31–33).

Jesus refers to two becoming one flesh in Matthew 19:4–6, which is a Scripture frequently used in marriage ceremonies around the world.

Although marriage is not for everyone, I for one love being married! If you aren't married and hope to be, keep reading and prayerfully what you learn from this chapter will be preparation.

In the beginning, God created all those wonderful things in the garden, and then in Genesis 2:18, He said, "It is not good for the man to be alone. I will make a helper suitable for him." Adam and Eve were created for each other. In Genesis 2:24, we see that marriage was designed by God, a gift to Adam and Eve: "That is why a man leaves his father and mother and is united to his wife, and they become one flesh." Marriage is a gift!

Unfortunately we — you and I — don't live in a beautiful, tranquil, perfect garden. We live in the real world called the 21st century, which can be compared to a Hefty trash bag. We stuff it full — and then some — before the plastic is stretched so much it screams, *Enough! I can't take (no mo') anymore!* Sad, but true — with children to care for, homes to clean, errands to run, and meals to prepare, the idea of *romance* often is lost or pushed so far down the to-do list that it rarely makes it to the top. And is anyone else tired? No wonder it's hard to find time for intimacy.

When was the last time you did something special for your husband because you wanted to honor him? If you can't remember, it's been too long! Maybe you have a smile on your face because just recently you did something especially for him. Good job!

GOD CREATED MAN

God created man from the dust of the ground and evidently added a high level of testosterone. (I hope you're smiling.) Just moments after seeing Eve, Adam said, "Wo-man!" Therefore, when we consider our husbands' sexual desires, we simply must be aware that this is an area that we (the wife) alone can fulfill. Notice, man was made from dirt, while the woman was *fashioned* from his rib. Maybe that is the reason most women love fashion.

GOD'S IDEA FROM THE BEGINNING

Sex is one of God's greatest gifts. It is intended for the purposes of intimacy, pleasure, and procreation within the boundary of marriage. It is to be cherished, guarded, and is an act that celebrates the union of marriage. In fact, true love affects the heart, mind, and body. Just how significant is intimacy in marriage? Very! When two people fall in love, they begin to blend together. This is called *fusion*, where two become one. Although you are two very distinct people, marriage unites you, fuses you together. By design, God is the only glue that bonds people together. Without the "God glue," couples flounder, limp, and wobble as they desperately try to hold it all together. Thus the explanation, "Marriage is hard work!" With physical intimacy being an essential part of God's plan for marriage, you can see why married women, who get their identity from God Himself, can be both godly *and* sensual.

The institution of marriage has these basic parts:

- The man leaves his parents and, in a public act, promises himself to his wife.
- The man and woman are joined together by taking responsibility for each other's welfare and by loving the mate above all others.
- The two become one flesh in the intimacy and commitment of sexual union that is reserved for marriage.

The best marriages — the ones that sail past all the storms and clouds of life — include all three.

COULD IT BE SATAN?

Because of his wicked desire to destroy marriage, Satan has saturated our culture with a devastating sexual immorality. For some, he has twisted what God created for good into a tense, self-seeking, and cheap act, turning love into lust. His cheap trick often gives sex a dirty and perverted image. In this sex-crazed world the media has *gone wild,* so to speak. Consider what you see and read on magazine covers, what you hear in movies, what flashes across your computer screen. New advances in technology guarantee the continued significant growth of immorality. For more than a decade now, I've encouraged students to *save sex* for marriage, knowing God's plan is best. Be careful, little eyes, what you see, ears what you hear, and mouth what you say. I can assure you this message is equally as important for adults, both married and single alike.

SEX SELLS

Knowing that I was preparing to speak at a marriage retreat, my husband, Bruce, brought home a piece of mail he had received at work. He handed it to me and said, "Look at this."

I glanced at it, saw the sexy-looking lady on the front, who was wearing an itsy bitsy black bikini, and I said, "That's trashy! Who would advertise a restaurant with a half-naked woman on the front? They're sure not going to get my business."

Bruce said, "Chandra! That's the point. If you were a bit more observant, you would see they don't want your business, they want mine!" As he pointed out all the sexual innuendos, I couldn't believe what I had missed.

It is a well-known fact that when God created man, he made him very visual, and there it was, right in front of me, *the proof in the pudding.* Let me try to explain what I saw. The purpose: I want you to be aware of Satan's evil schemes to destroy *your* marriage.

- FIRST — It was mailed to a business, not a home.
- SECOND — On one side was a picture of a delicious-looking, hot, steaming steak, a baked potato topped with cheddar cheese, and green garnishing. Talk about tempting your appetite. The picture was so realistic, you could almost taste it! Sitting above the garnishing was a faint sketch of a *naked lady,* similar to the ones you see on truckers' mud flaps. Of course I missed that, but Bruce didn't.
- THIRD — *Complimentary lunch?* You and I both know nothing is free (except the grace we receive from our Savior). In the background was written *Glamour Girls.* They may have been giving food away, but believe me, the price would be through the roof by the time the meal was over.

- FOURTH — A list of drinks with very provocative names which I cannot share. My mouth hung open as Bruce pointed out the seductive details on the flyer. I was blushing just reading the words. Needless to say, I felt very naive and a little disgusted that this trashy ad had caught the eye of Bruce, my godly and committed husband.

The next morning I received an email from Bruce that read:

Chandra:

I tossed and turned last night and could not sleep. As I lay awake, I made some mental notes about that men's club advertisement:
- *Satan is in the advertising business.*
- *His mission — I come to kill, steal, and destroy:*
- *To Kill his appetite for his spouse.*
- *To Steal his relationship.*
- *To Destroy his marriage.*
- *His method — A way to a man's heart is through his eyes and his stomach.*
I love you and pray for our marriage every single day.

The most blessed man in the world,
Bruce

The marketing industry uses seductive ads to get our attention, and it's working. Fortunes are made each year, billions of dollars from those who have bought in, hook, line, and sinker. The key word . . . *sinker*! Like a car dangerously spinning out of control, wrecking everything in its path, this immoral scheme is wrecking lives, marriages, homes, and families every day!

The Father in Proverbs 5 tells his son to listen carefully to his wise counsel. That the lips of an immoral woman are as sweet as honey and her mouth is smoother than oil. The result is as bitter as poison, sharp as a double-edged sword. (vv. 1–4)

Satan knows how to dazzle us, finding the open space, one we've left unguarded, to slither his way into our hearts.

IT'S AN UGLY REALITY!

"Sex" is almost always used in the negative, referring to an unrestrained, lustful sexual appetite which is always wrong and ungodly. Unfortunately for some married couples, the world has perverted God's beautiful gift of sex in such a way, that it has distorted not only their views, but their sense of God-given sensuality. Church Lady, wake up! If you are married, you should be sensual and sexy, at least occasionally!

My second challenge for you: the next time you contemplate a midafternoon rendezvous with your husband . . . DO IT! Call him and tell him you have a surprise waiting for him when he gets in. Greet him at the door wearing that favorite dress or outfit that he loves you to wear. Set a table for two at dinner. Light some candles. Play romantic music. Give him a massage. Rub his feet.

ME BE SEDUCTIVE?

While speaking to a group of women on this subject, a woman said, "I don't think Christian ladies need to talk about these things, especially not at church."

"Are you familiar with the Song of Solomon?" I asked.

She replied, "There's no need to read that book; it's about private things."

There was a moment of silence and then everyone began to chuckle, and then the room was filled with laughter. Even this sweet little lady who felt uncomfortable about the subject was now wiping tears of laughter from the corners of her eyes.

God used this lady to confirm the need to start a dialogue with Church Ladies about His plan for intimacy *in* marriage. That's also the danger of the *here a book, there a book* way so many Christians read the Bible. Every book is inspired by God. Every book is important! Every book has something to teach believers.

My point — Church Ladies need to take care of their church man.

Four important words every wife needs to think of when pleasing her husband are:

- EYES — What does he see when he looks at you?
- EARS — What are you telling him, whispering in his ears?
- NOSE — How does your bedroom smell? Your sheets? More importantly, how do you smell?
- MOUTH — There is something very sensual about the mouth. A kiss can turn a moment into a romantic evening.

GODLY ROLE MODELS

Chances are you have heard about the Proverbs 31 woman. While this woman's life demonstrates the importance of wisdom, skills, and great compassion — overall the importance of godly character — there is another woman in the Bible that I'd like to introduce you to. The Bride of Solomon is a woman I believe every Church Lady, especially those who are married, should get to know.

King Solomon himself shares their beautiful story, from the days of courtship, to the wedding day and night. The book also talks about times of indifference, where a lack of intimacy brings distance to the couple. We see that marriage is sacred and that intimacy and lovemaking are of the essence to keep the relationship growing and alive.

As we read the bride's poetic words to describe Solomon, her lover, they capture us and draw us in. We discover sexual intimacy and marriage are put in their proper, God-given perspective when we read the dialogue between Solomon and his bride. If you haven't read Song of Solomon, you must! Let me warn you, the romance is pretty steamy.

KEEP THE ROMANCE ALIVE!

After telling a few of my "godly" girlfriends that I would be mentioning "signals" in my book, I received a few anonymous notes in my mail box by the end of that week:

> "After over 20 years of marriage, my husband and I can read each other like a book. After some flirting, he'll put on *his sexy smelling, make me want to melt, I'll do anything* cologne. Then he'll give me a hug, brush his neck up against me, but . . . he won't kiss me. That's when I know . . . we'll be playing in the sheets tonight!" — Anonymous

> "We have secret words, code for, 'let's make love', regardless of when and where we are." — Mysterious

> "'My lover is mine and I am his,' whispered or mouthed across a crowded room or from his recliner in the family room." — Anonymous

"We have a secret code — Hot and Spicy. Although we use it to imply food, we are both very aware of the hidden meaning."
— Spicy Mama

"My husband and I are in our late sixties and although we don't have sex very often, intimacy is still very much alive. Holding hands, taking walks, back rubs, and snuggling in bed is important."
— Grandy

THE POWER OF LOVE

Imagine you're lying in bed, reading a good book, resting your mind after a long day. Your husband is getting out of the shower when he begins his routine. He brushes his teeth, sprays on his deodorant, splashes on his cologne, and within moments he makes his grand entrance with nothing on but a grin. As he makes his way toward you, he has one thing on his mind — you pulling him ever-so close, whispering seductive words in his ear...and so on.

Instead while he walks toward you, you tilt your head slightly down, raise your eyes just over the brim of your glasses, and you think to yourself, *Please, put some clothes on!* Godly wife that you are, and being completely aware that you need to take care of your man, without hesitation you recite the words from Solomon's bride (Song of Solomon 2:5): "*Strengthen me with raisins, refresh me with apples, for I am faint with love.*"

LET'S REVERSE THE ROLE

You spend an hour preparing for your seductive entrance: showering, or perhaps taking a hot bubble bath, shaving your legs to assure they are smooth to his touch, considering what to wear or to wear nothing at all. You lather on the anti-age and firmness cream with hopes it will camouflage your upper knee area that now sags a bit in your more mature years. You spray on perfume (the one that makes him growl), shake your hair, and slowly make your entrance like a lioness carefully observing her prey.

If he hasn't fallen asleep by now, his eyes widen as he looks at you from head to toe, thinking, *Your body is a wonderland. That cellulite you worried about...what cellulite?* His eyes move across your body and then into your eyes, he pulls you close and says,

"How beautiful are your sandaled feet, O queenly maiden. Your rounded thighs are like jewels, the work of a skilled craftsman. Your navel is perfectly formed like a goblet filled with mixed wine. Between your thighs lies a mound of wheat bordered with lilies. Your breasts are like two fawns, twin fawns of a gazelle. Your neck is as beautiful as an ivory tower. Your eyes are like the sparkling pools in Heshbon by the gate of Bath-Rabbim. Your nose is as fine as the tower of Lebanon overlooking Damascus. Your head is as majestic as Mount Carmel, and the sheen of your hair radiates royalty" (Song of Solomon 7:1–5, NLT).

OK. OK. I'll stop right there! Whew! Somebody get me a fan . . . please!

Take my advice, if you want to spice things up in the bedroom, light some candles and bring your Bible to bed. Together read the poetic words found in Song of Solomon. Let me warn you that you might not get much reading done.

DATE NIGHT

If you aren't already scheduling "one-on-one" time with your husband, it's never too late to start! Consider this your reminder: *Make time for date night!* You don't need a lot of money. Be creative! Dates don't have to be at night, take major planning, or be expensive.

- Take a walk in the park.
- Take a Sunday drive.
- Get ice cream and eat it there.
- Find a new place for lunch or dinner.
- Plan a romantic evening at home; take the children somewhere else.

Solomon's bride didn't wait for her husband to seduce her; instead she initiated the romance. She woke him up early in the morning and she took him out to the vineyards, where they made love. Yes! Right there in the vineyard! You can see the freedom in their marriage as it had matured:

I belong to my beloved, and his desire is for me. Come, my beloved, let us go to the countryside, let us spend the night in the villages. Let us go early to the vineyards to see if the vines have budded, if their blossoms have opened, and if the pomegranates are in bloom—there I will give you my love. The mandrakes send out their fragrance, and at our door is every delicacy, both new and old, that I have stored up for you, my beloved. (Song of Solomon 7:10–13)

God continues to teach me that men are wired differently by His design. As women, we need to do our best to understand our husband better, so we can take care of his needs more effectively.

Satan has done a first-class job distorting God's plan for sex to the *unmarried*, with an "if it feels good, do it" attitude, making sex with two consenting adults outside of marriage seem natural and an OK thing to do — of course, not to mention the emotional, physical, and spiritual consequences that come with premarital sex.

On the other hand, his clever tactics have also twisted and perverted "sex" to the point that words such as *sexy* and *sensual* seem ungodly to some Church Ladies, while their husbands are craving more "sexy" in their marriage. Unbelievable! Satan's evil plan has hit two birds with one stone, causing severe damage to both the unmarried and married Church Lady.

Church Ladies — instead of being unresponsive and caught off guard tomorrow, we need to stand guard like soldiers on the frontlines today; to become warriors who constantly pray for our marriages, our husbands, and our families. Perhaps it's time to take off that "everything is wonderful" façade we sometimes wear and admit we are under attack! Guard your post! No one else will stand guard like you can.

GODLY AND SENSUAL WIFE TEST

How often do you:
- Flirt with your husband?
- Plan special things just for him?
- Show gratitude for all he does or simply for the way he loves you?
- Affirm him and build him up with words?
- Make him feel significant?

When was the last time you:
- Initiated the romance?
- Made his lunch and put a love note in the bag?
- Took a shower with him?
- Did that one thing that he loves you to do . . . just because?
- Surprised him?

Jesus said, "So in everything, do to others what you would have them do to you" (Matthew 7:12).

JUST A LITTLE TIP

What does your bedroom look like? A wise woman once told me that the master bedroom should represent the marriage and be the room where both the husband and the wife can relax — a place of tranquility. It *should be* warm and inviting, an escape, your romantic getaway, a place where you have private talks; give much love, and in return, receive much love.

The decor *should not* be too terribly feminine or masculine, but instead have a romantic flare that fits the two of you. There *should not* be deer or elk heads mounted on the walls . . . and you can tell your hunter husbands that I said this! (Unless, however, you both agree that animal heads and skins are romantic; you never know. I guess I should not assume.)

It *should not* be where all the clothes end up at the end of the day, or where the children play. Books and bills should not be cluttered or untidy on the floor or bedside table. Seeing those stressful items can blow the flame right out of any romantic night.

Never forget — there are no winners and losers in marriage. If one wins, you both win. If one loses, you both lose. Remember you are "one."

After reading this chapter, my prayer is that date night, the master bedroom, and intimacy within your marriages will ignite; that romance in the life of the Church Lady who calls herself *Mrs.* will be more passionate and giving; and that Christian marriages will benefit greatly as they honor God more!

Recognizing there are many different stories, different ideas, different cultures, my examples may not apply to every Church Lady who reads this. There are countless conditions that may make my applications invalid. Example: wives and husbands who have medical concerns, handicaps; those who live in abusive situations; as well as other circumstances that I may not have mentioned. If this includes you, don't allow Satan to bamboozle your thoughts, causing guilt or hurt feelings. Be creative; find ways to keep the intimacy alive and well. Talk to your husband about his feelings as you share your own. Marriage is based on love.

> *Love is patient and kind. Love is not jealous or boastful or proud or rude. It does not demand its own way. It is not irritable, and it keeps no record of being wronged. It does not rejoice about injustice but rejoices whenever the truth wins out. Love never gives up, never loses faith, is always hopeful, and endures through every*

circumstance. Three things will last forever — faith, hope, and love — and the greatest of these is love" (1 Corinthians 13:4–7, 13 *NLT*).

INTENTIONAL DEVOTION

Surely there are ladies reading this that may have a dark past; it is Satan's attempt to bring up guilt, certainly not our heavenly Father's. Everyone has a past! Say these words out loud: *Everyone has a past!* Stop looking back; look forward instead! Romans 5:8–9 says this:

> *But God showed his great love for us by sending Christ to die for us while we were still sinners. And since we have been made right in God's sight by the blood of Christ, he will certainly save us from God's condemnation.*

Do you understand what that means? You and I have been restored! God loves you with intentional devotion and, being confident that He forgives confessed sin, don't walk in shame. Instead hold your head high. Allow His unconditional love to be poured over you like a mighty rushing waterfall, washing you whiter than snow through the saving grace of His Son, Jesus Christ, who died so that you would live — and in freedom, I must add.

If you are experiencing darkness and pain, heartache in your marriage even now, allow God to embrace you. Search His Word for inspiration, for wisdom, and for encouragement. Find a godly mentor, someone you can speak freely with, pray with, and trust. Let me encourage you: don't be so quick to give up on your marriage. Marriage is more than a feeling, it's a commitment, and needs unconditional love. Remember, there are no perfect people. Not your husband and not you! Only God is perfect and He loves you with a perfect love.

Write these on a sticky note and put them in a place you look daily. Tips for a happy, healthy, and loving marriage, in this order are: 1) To know and Love God — a personal relationship with Jesus Christ, reading the Bible, prayer 2) To love and support your husband 3) Love him unconditionally, do special things for him, honor him 4) To communicate effectively — no secrets — talk about his day and yours, share dreams for the future.

Pray and ask the Lord to give you the desire to honor your husband in what you say and what you do! If this is difficult because you have hurt and bitterness toward him, ask the Lord to help you forgive him, to bring intimacy back to your marriage again.

The key is having a Christ-centered marriage. When couples independently have a relationship with Jesus Christ, His love sweetens the relationship, which most assuredly sweetens the intimacy. Do you honor God first and always? Do you honor your husband?

*P*RAYER

Heavenly Father, You know the heart of the one who reads this. You know her every need. I pray that the words above have encouraged her, whatever her situation. If she has been abused, mistreated, betrayed, unloved, and certainly not honored, may she find comfort in Your love today. Lord, may this Church Lady be filled up to overflowing with your joy. Give her a new love and passion for her husband and let her husband notice and begin to honor her. Heal her hurt and begin to restore her relationship with her husband.

If on the other hand she has a godly husband who provides, loves, and honors her, may she never take him for granted. Bless him for his faithfulness and obedience according to Your Holy Word. Continue to bless their marriage.

Lord, if this Church Lady needed this reminder because she has failed to honor her husband — perhaps she has grown distant and they've become more like roommates than lovers — awaken her spirit. Give her a fresh desire to love her husband intimately again. Bring to her mind why she fell in love with him in the first place.

Thank You for the gift of marriage and intimacy. Forgive us when we allow busyness, the kids, and the to-do list to keep us from physically loving our husband. May this be a reminder for us to slow down, get our priorities in order, and to take out some of those things we've forced into our schedule that keep us too busy and too tired to be both godly and sensual. Lord, renew our passion and refresh our desire to honor our husbands. Amen.

*R*EVEAL AND *T*RANSFORM

I. Take a moment to pray for your marriage.
   - Thank the Lord for your marriage.
   - Ask the Lord to take any wrongs and make them right.
   - If you have lost that loving feeling, ask the Lord to ignite it again.

- If you are holding onto past hurts, give them to Jesus today.
- Ask the Lord to reveal those areas where you can be a better wife.

2. Are you or your husband more giving in these areas?
   - Time
   - Words of affirmation
   - Gifts
   - Touch

3. After reading this chapter, have you been challenged to make any changes? Explain.

4. Has the world's perverted view of *sex* had any impact on your or your husband's view of sex? How?

5. Describe your dream date.

6. Finish this statement: If I were to plan a romantic day, evening, or getaway, I would ...

7. What do you often wish your husband would do?

8. What do you think he wishes you would do?

9. How has the gift of marriage blessed you? Depending on your answers, you may want to be careful what you write that others may see. However, look for an opportunity to share what you have written with your husband.

10. If you are not married yet, or don't have the desire to get married, what will you take from this chapter?

CHAPTER 6

Lasting Impressions

Never be lazy, but work hard and serve the Lord enthusiastically.

— ROMANS 12:11 (NLT)

I'm sure you know her — the lady in your church who, without a spoken word, is clearly a Church Lady. She is gentle, kind, and as ladylike as one can be. Perhaps it was her that came to your mind when you first saw the title of this book. The room illuminates when she enters. Godliness oozes out of her. Well, she would never use the word *ooze*, but you get the picture, right? If she were to describe something that oozes, she would say, "her cup *runneth* over." And she would never say, "Hello, I'm the Church Lady." Humility is her gift. In fact, it's not what she says at all, but *whose* she is that makes her so special. Everyone knows she loves the heavenly Father, fears the Lord, and is highly aware of His holiness. Let's agree there are no perfect people, but this lady is the epitome of the Church Lady — joy, peace, and love adorn her.

We can't talk about Church Ladies without mentioning that woman of godly character we know as the Proverbs 31 woman. This woman has strong character, wisdom, grace, the love and respect of her husband, and her children call her blessed. She cares for others, has good foresight, and she is also good with money — and the one thing that encompasses her whole life is that she fears the Lord God. What lady wouldn't want to have these words said of her? She is, after all, the ideal woman, right? I don't know about you, but she seems a little unrealistic to me. After all, Proverbs 31:10 begins with these words: "The wife of noble character, *who can find?*" Whew! I feel better already! I've always wondered, *Where is this lady?*

I can't help but think how the author of Proverbs might describe her today. The character and godliness of this noble woman would surely remain the same; however, the author may describe her daily qualities quite differently. Just for fun, let me share with you what I think the author might say:

She is worth far more than rubies and diamonds. Her husband has confidence in her, and can be assured she will greet him at the door (no matter how busy or chaotic her day has been), well dressed and with a kiss when he arrives home from his hard day at work. She brings him good, not harm, always builds him up and encourages him; she would never put him down in front of others, all the days of his life.

She shops at discount stores and finds treasures, dressing her family in a trendy yet conservative and modest fashion. Her teenage daughters adore all that she does for them, and they have dreams of being just like Mom. Her sons are so appreciative of their mother; they greet her with a kiss in front of their friends and remove their shoes before entering the house. Oh-so obedient.

She arises early each day, going to stores both near and far to find the freshest meats and organic vegetables, being sure to have something everyone in her family likes for dinner. Her selections indeed make everyone happy as they sit around the table promptly at six. She serves a well-rounded and healthy dinner each night, of course, never thinking of having dinner delivered. She properly sets the table with fabric napkins, her best dishes, silverware, and matching glassware, and she lights tapered candles for the perfect ambiance. She always makes extra food to take to the neighbors, delivering the meal in plastic bowls so they wouldn't be burdened to wash and return them.

When she drives by land for sale that meets the real-estate priority — location, location, location — she makes the purchase and begins to till the land the following day, so that planting can begin immediately. Her husband never has to ask her twice, and can count on her knowledge to get the job done.

She never spends too much money on herself. She colors and cuts her own hair and does her own nails. She never makes a purchase on a credit card, keeps all the household finances in place, always has time to help the children with projects and homework, and somehow always looks radiant at the end of the day.

After she tucks everyone safely into bed, saying prayers with each one, she is sure to check that all the doors are locked, the coffee pot is ready for the next morning, and that her children's clothes are laid out, while being sure that her husband's shirt is pressed and ready. Lunches are made in the refrigerator; each one has the sandwich of choice ready to go with the creatively written name on the front of the bag, which also has a handwritten note of encouragement along with a Bible verse signed, "With Love, Your Praying Mother."

OK! BACK TO REALITY!

By the way, if you do, or have ever done any of the tasks mentioned above, kudos to you! I just had to pat myself (and you) on the back before Satan dealt the guilt card on us.

Now, some ladies have crossed my path who do have the traditional Church Lady qualities. Example: never late and never in a hurry; always well put together, with a fragrance that lingers in the air long after she has gone; her eloquent, soft-spoken words seem to draw the attention of every ear when she speaks; she always stands out in a crowd, although she never intentionally brings attention to herself; she fears the Lord, and everyone genuinely respects her. Maybe like me, you too have had the wonderful privilege of rubbing shoulders with a few of these precious ladies who have been great role models.

Thinking back, there were several who made a huge impression on my life at an early age. I can still remember what they looked like, and I know them by name. While I share about these who left lasting impressions on my life, I pray that you too will recall those who touched your life as well.

BIBLE TEACHER

When I was in third grade, my Sunday School teacher, Mrs. Stovall, gave me a beautiful white Bible with my name on the front cover for my birthday. I was so proud of that big Bible. I remember Bible drill at the beginning of Sunday School every Sunday. I would flip the pages back and forth from the Old Testament to the New. It was Mrs. Stovall that taught me there were 66 books in the Bible — 39 in the Old Testament, and 27 in the New Testament. She taught me songs about the books of the Bible that I still recall to this day. Isn't it amazing how we don't forget things we were taught so long ago? Hmm, the Bible does say something about how the Word never returns void. Mrs. Stovall knew that promise too!

There are people whose influence makes a huge impact on our lives. I was fortunate and blessed that at a young age, I was impacted not only by my godly mother but many other Church Ladies too. Mrs. Stovall always dressed beautifully and smelled like fresh-cut flowers. The scent of magnolia seems to be what I remember. Everyone loved her. She was a woman who feared the Lord, and all those who knew Mrs. Stovall loved and respected her.

For we are to God the pleasing aroma of Christ (2 Corinthians 2:15).

MISSIONARY

When I got a little older, I participated in Girls in Action® (GA®) on Wednesday night — otherwise known in the Baptist Church as Wednesday Night Discipleship. A great deal of our Bible study time was based on the Great Commission: "Go into all the world and preach the gospel to all creation. Whoever believes and is baptized will be saved, but whoever does not believe will be condemned" (Mark 16:15–16).

We learned about missionaries and every week prayed for those who had a birthday. Going to GA camp for weekend retreats is where I met Mildred McWhorter. I thought she was famous! She not only spoke to us at GA camp, but she ran the mission home (orphanage) in downtown Houston, Texas, for years. We would go there several times a year to help her feed the homeless and to clean up the orphanage where she served.

I remember she was funny, and that her love for Jesus could not be contained. Something about her reminded me of Mrs. Claus — you know, as in Santa Claus, but she was real! Mrs. McWhorter loved to talk about Jesus. She told us that Jesus was her best friend, and she could talk to Him anytime she wanted. She would tell us, "You can talk to Jesus too. He's always with you. Just pretend He is sitting right there beside you when you talk." She also taught me that skin color didn't make a difference to Jesus. She lived what she taught, and she loved all of us the same. The kids who lived in poverty were treated no different than the church kids who came to serve. I can almost hear her now: "Together we can make a greater difference for the kingdom. Red and yellow, black and white, they are *all* precious in His sight!" Mrs. McWhorter gave her life serving others. She taught me so much about the Bible and the Lord because of what she did, not just by what she said.

> *Do nothing out of selfish ambition or vain conceit. Rather, in humility value others above yourselves, not looking to your own interests but each of you to the interests of the others. In your relationships with one another, have the same mindset as Christ Jesus.* (Philippians 2:3–5)

Mildred McWhorter knew her worth in God's kingdom. She treated everyone with great respect and love. She was a true reflection of Jesus. She was one of a kind. She was a Church Lady!

JOY!

Then there was Mrs. Wanda Kipp. So fun! She had this laugh that made everyone around her laugh. Her smile was simply an expression of God's love that flowed out of her heart. "I can't keep it inside, I have to share my joy with others," she would tell us. We were friends, even though she was much older than me. I even learned to write my name the way she wrote it because her handwriting was so beautiful. She made the C larger than all the other letters, and it curved under half my name. I still write my name like that to this day.

She could sing like a bird. She taught me that integrity and godly character are very important in life. "A person's eyes and smile tell you a lot about them," she taught us. Mrs. Kipp taught me that Christians need to laugh. I can hear her now: "Little girls and grown-up ladies that belong to Jesus should always be smiling. Just practice this: **J**esus, **O**thers, and then **Y**ourself. That's how you experience real JOY in your heart."

How grateful I am that Mrs. Kipp taught me the importance of laughter and fun! She taught me that with Jesus you can have joy in all circumstances. She was right! She lives her life to reflect Jesus, and it's contagious! Like the flu in the middle of influence, I caught it! *I have told you this so that my joy may be in you and that your joy may be complete* (John 15:11).

Mrs. McWhorter, Mrs. Stovall, and Mrs. Kipp . . . yes, they were the first in my mind to be given the title of the Church Lady. They were the real deal. They were role models for me and so many others. These Church Ladies left a lasting impression on my life.

When they get to heaven, if people really line up to thank those who influenced them to trust and believe in Jesus, these lines would be some of the longest, I'm sure. The funny thing is, the role models would be oblivious that they have a line. They would just be asking, "Where is He? Where is Jesus?" Now, that's a Church Lady!

There will never be another Mrs. Stovall — she was beautiful and an incredible example of the Proverbs 31 woman. There will never be another Mrs. McWhorter — she was a great teacher, missionary, and had a servant heart. Mrs. Kipp — I have never met another like her. She loved to laugh and sing, and her cup . . . it was filled with joy. Each of these ladies had unique qualities and lived an authentic life! These ladies had an intimate relationship with Jesus; therefore, they reflected that love to me. Like putty in His hand, they gave their lives to God, so that He could shape and chisel them as He needed to. Wherever they are today, I am confident they are still impacting the lives of others as they continue to serve the Lord. And if they are already in Heaven, I bet you could find them at the feet of Jesus, worshiping and praising Him. What a blessing to have these precious Church Ladies leave a lasting impression on my life.

ONE OF A KIND

God is teaching me a lot about the Church Ladies. I see them everywhere! They all look different — sometimes traditional, other times nontraditional. Some are older than me, others my age, while others are much younger than me. Sometimes I see a Church Lady who reminds me of Mrs. Stovall — beautiful feminine suit, hair styled perfectly, speaking with Scripture that seems to roll out of her mouth. Other times I am reminded of my new friend Madison (whom I mentioned in chap. 2) with permanent artwork all over her body. God uses different types of ladies to share His message, different types of ladies reaching the needs of different kinds of people with His love, for His people, for His glory, all for His purpose. Amazingly, with all our differences, the love of Christ within us seems to draw us to one another.

Think of your closest friends, your family, your church, your work, your community, your city, your state, your country. Now think bigger: the continents you can name, the countries you can't . . . the world! God loves the world! How much?

> *This is how much God loved the world: He gave his Son, his one and only Son. And this is why: so that no one need be destroyed; by believing in him, anyone can have a whole and lasting life. God didn't go to all the trouble of sending his Son merely to point an accusing finger, telling the world how bad it was. He came to help, to put the world right again.* (John 3:16–17 *The Message*)

Notice he *didn't* say, "So the rich, the famous, the well dressed, well-groomed, those who live in a specific kind of neighborhood, drive a particular car, have obedient children, etc." Nor did he say just for the poor, the depressed, the homeless, the abused, the uneducated. No. He didn't name a specific name because he never wanted there to be a question. For God so loved the *whole world*. That includes you! You see, we are the ones who categorize and group people, not Him. We think just because someone has money, has a lot of friends, and lives in a nice house, they are so lucky — oops, the Church Lady would say, "*So blessed.*" Unfortunately, many of those women who seem to have it all together on the outside may have a home life you would never trade yours for. Or they may have heartache that is deep, secrets that must be kept, guilt that keeps them walking in shame, all keeping them from living a life of freedom, ultimately keeping them from experiencing real joy.

I'm thankful for all the Church Ladies God has put in my path. Although we are different, we are much the same. Material possessions, popularity, higher education, kept traditions, being at the top of the ladder, fame and fortune, taking fancy vacations, and driving fine cars don't always equal a happy life — it is no secret! If you lack all that I have listed above, but you have Jesus, you will experience real joy. Happiness comes and goes. Real joy comes from a relationship with Jesus Christ, which enables us to have a relationship with God the Father. These wise Church Ladies from my past knew that teaching godly principles to this little girl would set the foundation for the rest of my life. These Church Ladies left a lasting impression which has greatly impacted my life and will continue to impact my future. There is nothing greater than sharing the love of Jesus. That, in the end, is truly all that really matters.

How wonderful that God uses others to mold us and shape us into the one-of-a-kind women He has purposed us to be. How exciting to know there are many Church Ladies who are walking beside us on this journey, each one changing us a bit so that we reflect Him more.

I have to admit, the Church Lady looks a lot different to me at 48 than she did when I was 5 years old — or a teenager, for that matter. She's not old! Look in the mirror and see for yourself.

WHO'S WATCHING YOU?

Pressing "rewind" on my life has been good. There have been many who have touched my life: Sunday School teachers, youth workers, pastors, friends, aunts, and especially my mom and dad. Those snapshots will forever be ingrained on my mind. I am grateful to each one who has poured into my life, some knowingly and others who were just living the life of a believer.

I have to wonder who is watching me and you. Are there little girls, teenagers, your children, neighbors to consider? Believe me, others are watching how we live our life, what we say, and what we do. What kind of impression are we leaving on their lives? Have we been a positive influence on others? Even today, have we been a blessing to someone, somewhere?

Let me encourage you to be the best you that God designed you to be. Let's stop trying to fit the mold of some other Church Lady. God broke that mold, just like He broke the mold after He made you. That's not just a pickup line, or something your daddy once said — it's true! Stop trying to conform to other people; stop thinking about what they have and what you don't; how their body is shaped and how yours . . . well, it is not! When I consider these ladies who have left such a lasting impression on my life, not one of them came close to looking alike or having the same gifts and talents as the others.

Let's consider my mom. When I was a teenager, I remember wishing that my mom was more like this friend's mom or that one's. Now that I'm a mom, I appreciate the one-of-a-kind mom that she was and still is today. Thank you, Mom, for just being you, and for leaving a godly legacy for me. I'm passing all that you taught me onto my girls, and to girls and women around the world. Prayerfully, they too will keep this worthwhile tradition going, leaving a lasting impression for generations to come.

But thanks be to God, who [. . .] uses us to spread the aroma of the knowledge of him everywhere. For we are to God the pleasing aroma of Christ among those who are being saved and those who are perishing. To the one we are an aroma that brings death; to the other, an aroma that brings life." (2 Corinthians 2:14–16)

Reveal and Transform

1. Who came to your mind immediately when you read *the Church Lady*? Why?

2. Can you identify the thread of particular Church Ladies woven in the tapestry of your life today?

3. Who had the greatest influence on your Christian life?

4. Even with her flaws, is there one you knew who was particularly hard on you, perhaps even judgmental, but now you can see how God used her influence to make you the person you are today?

5. Who are those who have crossed your path for only a moment, but greatly influenced you? All in all, consider those who have shown the love of Christ to you on this journey so far in your life.

6. On the timeline provided, beginning with the first time you remember hearing about Jesus Christ, chart the major influences to date (heard about Jesus, accepted Jesus as Savior, etc.).

7. Who are you able to influence daily?

8. Are there any changes you need to make on what people see you do or hear you say?

9. If you could talk to one Church Lady, to say thank you, who would it be? Call her. Send a note or perhaps a copy of this book. Let her know how grateful you are for her Christian influence on your life.

10. Pray. Ask the Lord to reveal and transform you to reflect Him more so others always see Christ in you.

CHAPTER 7

The Whine Club

Rejoice in our confident hope.
Be patient in trouble, and keep on praying.

— ROMANS 12:12 (NLT)

Do you have any Debbie Downers in your life? Know any whiners? These people can wear you down, suck the life right out of you. They are a chore to be around. The whiner may say, "Thank you for being a good listener," but the truth is, you're listening because you don't have anything to say. You're thinking to yourself, *What petty complaining*, or perhaps, *How immature!* And maybe even, *It never seems to stop with this girl.*

Whine — go on about, moan, bellyache, and gripe. To complain in an unreasonable, repeated, or irritating way. Children do this often to get what they want.

OK, let's be honest. How many times have you been the one whining? Me too!

If we're really honest, there are times when we all need someone to whine to. None of us want to be known as a whiner, so if you are an occasional whiner, you're just being real, but please, don't make it a habit or become someone that does it just to get attention. It's not very ladylike, and certainly not godly! Then there's the question, *Who can I whine to?* My husband is my best friend, but he will tune me out if I start to whine. That's why sometimes we need a girlfriend to share with. Besides, even the Bible says it is better to live in the desert than *with a crabby, complaining wife* (Proverbs 21:19).

Like every woman, we Church Ladies need to have at least one girl-friend that is godly, has a good reputation, is trustworthy, *and* is a good listener. Or should I say, a friend that is willing to listen even when you whine. "There are friends who destroy each other, but a real friend sticks closer than a brother" (Proverbs 18:24 NLT). Depending on the circumstance, this friend may laugh with you, pray with you, cry with you, or perhaps speak the truth in love even when it's not what you really want to hear. Do you have a friend like this? If not, pray for one.

Honestly, the "whine club" that I'm speaking of does not include whiney people that we commonly think of as whiners, or the constant complaining type, and certainly not the whine of a gossip. No. The whine club that I belong to is one that gives honor to Jesus. Are you confused yet? Let me explain.

One night while driving to a Spurs game with three of my girlfriends, it dawned on me: every girl needs another girl to whine to. Since Ruth and Naomi, Mary and Martha, and Wilma and Betty, women have a need to share what is going on in their life. From the children, the husband, the good marriage and the bad, the tears, the pain, laughter and joy, discussing how body parts are changing and dropping or drooping lower, and of course, times when a hug and a simple prayer spoken is just what we need — every girl needs a safe place to whine.

On this particular night, it wasn't by chance we were together. Jill, my dear friend, had actually prayed about who she would give her three extra tickets to. If you enjoy NBA basketball, you may be thinking, *What a great idea for a girls' night out.* If you don't like basketball, it must be because you don't have a team as superior as the Spurs to cheer for. And I have to admit I love my Spurs! Go, Spurs, go! Whatever category you fall into, getting together for the game was really just a fun reason to get the girls together, and we had a suite at the Alamodome! Not too shabby! The four of us had known each other for years. Our kids had grown up together at church and at school, but they had all graduated by this time, and it had been over a year since we had a good, long visit. What we needed was a few hours to catch up. Little did we know the Lord was already at work and had an agenda of His own; I guess you could say this was a *divine appointment.* I would say, most definitely a safe place to whine.

After the hugs and giggly chitchat (girls will be girls, no matter their age) and small talk — you know, *How are you? How's Bruce? How are the girls?* — then we got to Robin and she said, "Well, do you really want to know?" Tears begin to fill her eyes like rising water in leaky goggles. She began to tell us what was going on in her life. She had been holding it in for months because she didn't want gossip to get out, admitting she had already taken all the hurt she could stand. Weary from the pressure of this heavy burden, she was desperate to share her hurt.

The night she got the call from Jill inviting her for a girls' night out, she felt it was God's plan all along. She shared how she had been very concerned about her oldest son whom she feared was not only taking drugs, but she was almost positive he was selling them too. Her younger son seemed to be going down the same path with drugs and alcohol, and as their mother, she was grieving their choices, asking the question, *Where did I go wrong?*

There was a long pause, she wiped a few tears from her face, and then she went on. She said, "And then, there's my marriage." The look on our faces as we listened more intently seemed to visualize what we were all thinking: *Could it get any worse?* She went on to tell us that her husband had announced he was seeing someone else, and therefore wanted out of the marriage.

Like being hit in the gut, the pain I felt for my friend had deflated every word out of me. What could I say? What could any of us say? Then there is love, genuine love that comes from only one source: the overflowing well of God's love. Listening was enough. Sometimes there just aren't words to speak, and that's OK — even best, at times, I suppose.

She expressed to us that she had been carrying around this load, giving it to Jesus each day, but needed desperately to share it face to face with trusted friends.

Needless to say, the froufrou "everything's going great" pretense was over and there was a real crisis to face. This was BIG! Yes, we are Church Ladies. Yes, we love Jesus! Yes, we fear God! So, how could this happen to one of us? *Because we are human.*

That sounds like such a lame excuse, doesn't it? How could a man who had been married to this godly and beautiful woman, have children with her, be a leader in his church, months earlier have celebrated their 20th anniversary, and then out of nowhere say, "I want a divorce!"? I don't understand it! Oh, but it happens more and more often than we want to admit. Robin expressed how she had been walking with her head down, feeling shame, even guilt somehow.

The hurt must be indescribable, I thought as I listened. So much hurt! Feeling betrayed by someone you love — it has to leave such a deep wound. The one man on earth she gave her hand in marriage to, made a vow with, a commitment to what she knew to be true in her heart, the one who she thought loved her in the very same way, the one who said he would be there with her in sickness and in health, till death do us part! Where did it go wrong? Had she done something to push him away? Was he no longer attracted to her? And if so, is that really a good enough reason to break the marriage vow? You can imagine the questions inside her mind, the hurt in her heart, the feelings of embarrassment and shame because she — a Christian woman — was on her way to divorce court. What would people say? It wasn't at all what she had planned, but it was out of her control.

Robin put her focus on the Lord in the midst of her agonizing pain. This strong, godly woman had been whipped to her knees, weak and discouraged, broken and bruised. It was who she knows (Jesus) that would sustain her. Her hope comes from the Lord! My friend was clinging to the promises of God, knowing full well she could trust Him when all else had failed her.

Listed below are Scripture references that give mercy, grace, and hope and who we are in Christ.

- I am chosen. — John 15:19
- I am justified and redeemed. — Romans 3:24
- I am holy and blameless in His sight. — Ephesians 1:4
- I am not condemned. — Romans 15:7
- I am strong in His power. — Ephesians 5:9
- I can do all things through Christ who gives me strength. — Philippians 4:13
- I am wonderfully made. — Psalm 139:14

CHRIST WAS BETRAYED

Jesus Himself was betrayed by two of His best friends, and suffered because of it. In Matthew 26, Jesus knew His life on earth was coming to an end. What God had Him come here to do was almost finished. Jesus Himself agonized as He prayed to the Father. Alone in the garden, He cried out, "My father, if it is not possible for this cup to be taken away unless I drink it, may Your will be done" (v. 39). Can you imagine His pain and heartache? He knew what He needed to do, and was willing to lay down His life; however, He loved us so much that He wanted to supply our greatest need.

Have you ever wished you could know your future? Maybe like me, you've thought, *if I could only have a peek into the future, perhaps I could be better prepared, making the suffering a little easier.* We have a great example of this. Jesus Himself knew what He was facing. He knew that He would be betrayed, and that He would soon leave this earth. However, when we read Matthew 26 and other accounts of His last days, we see that even in His obedience, there was anguish. Although Jesus was fully God in His humanity, we hear from the writer of Hebrews that He cried out to God, His Father, the One who could save Him from death: "During the days of Jesus' life on earth, he offered up prayers and petitions with fervent cries and tears to the one who could save him from death" (Hebrews 5:7). Jesus shared with His disciples, His closest friends, that one of them would betray Him (Matthew 26:21). And imagine the hurt He must have felt when Peter denied Him, not once, not twice, but three times (Matthew 26:34).

In this life, there will be trials and suffering, heartache and pain. But for those of us who put our trust in Jesus, we have a hope and a future. We know when we are weak that Jesus is strong. There is indeed a peace that passes all understanding, and that peace is found in Jesus Christ alone. It is His great love for us that keeps the raging storms of life from tossing us overboard. He keeps the boat of life steady, even in the middle of the storm. When we reach out our hand and call out the name of Jesus, His hand grips us tightly as He pulls us up out of the raging waters.

Consider the life of Jesus. Take a moment to ponder His first day on earth and His last. Then remember what Jesus was teaching right up to the moment He took his last breath.

During the 33 years He spent on the earth, every word spoken, every story and parable shared, every miracle witnessed, even the finger that touched the hem of His garment was destined, all for one purpose — to point us to the love of God the Father.

He said that even the Son of man did not come to be served, but to serve, and to give his life as a ransom for many (Mark 10:44–45).

No eye has seen, no ear has heard, and no mind has imagined
What God has prepared for those who love him. (1 Corinthians 2:9)

Let's reflect back: Isaiah had prophesied the Messiah would come from the descendants of David. For more than 400 hundred years from Isaiah's time, Jews were waiting for the Messiah to come (Luke 3). When Jesus Christ came into the world, His betrayal was immediate (Matthew 2:1–13). Herod, the king of the Jews, thought this child, Jesus, the supposed Messiah, wanted to take his throne. Herod was mistaken and quickly became so consumed with jealousy, anger, pride, and pure evil, that he didn't understand that Jesus wanted to be King of his heart, not claim his earthly throne. Jesus did come to be King, not because of the long lines on election day, but because God appointed Him as King — King of the world, King of heaven. Now you and I have a choice to make: will you make Him King of your heart, or not?

You see, this world has been a mess since that fateful day in the Garden of Eden. Did you know that *Jesus* means "the Lord saves"? Jesus came to seek and save the lost. And if Jesus Christ is Lord of your life, He is in control. Ask yourself, *Is Jesus Christ my Savior? Is Jesus Christ my Lord?* It seems strange, but it is true that many have made Jesus Savior, and by His grace, they've been given an eternal inheritance in heaven, but not all have made Jesus Lord, which gives Him control of our lives. In her song, "Jesus, Take the Wheel," Carrie Underwood's words say it well. The woman in the song has lost control and she says, "Here's my life, Jesus, You take charge. Jesus, take the wheel."

My sweet friend and sister in Christ, Robin, had made Jesus Lord of her life. Although she was in one of the most treacherous storms of her life, she trusted the Lord to keep her from drowning in the deep waters of a lake called *Suffering*. God proved to be faithful to Robin. She made it through the storm; once again she is sailing in calm waters.

Needless to say Robin's story opened the door for everyone to share, to be real, genuine, and authentic! Basketball game — what game? We sat up in the sky box and ate peanuts and pretzels and talked through the whole game.

By the sound of those first ten minutes together, who would have ever thought we would all have some kind of issue going on? But we did! Another friend began to share how her daughter was struggling with anxiety issues, and it had gotten to the point where she couldn't eat. She had kept this anxiety problem a secret because she didn't want people in the church to gossip about her daughter — or her parenting skills, for that matter. And she sure didn't want that added strain on her daughter, or on their mother-daughter relationship. She expressed with grief how sometimes prayer requests become what ignite the fires of gossip. Unfortunately, in some cases this is true. If you have a daughter, you can understand her reasoning.

Another shared how she was tired of keeping secrets from her past, her marriage, her home life. Although she didn't share the problems, we knew to pray.

The only thing I was struggling with was turning 45 and noticing my body was changing like crazy! The tears quickly turned into laughter as all four of us admitted the same changes. We discussed what panties don't show panty lines and how wonderful Spanx are, and someone mentioned a miracle cream that takes cellulite away. Don't worry yourself wondering what it was called, because it didn't work a miracle on my thighs!

On the way home from the game, one of the ladies said, "Thank you for letting me whine." Another quickly said, "Let's just call us the Whine Club!" We laughed again until we cried. Our night was so sweet. We ended our night with prayer, seeking God in each of our situations for help, for hope, and for healing.

For my friend Robin, and for others that I know who are hurting — perhaps even you — God has the power to work in the midst of your hurt, in the midst of your storm. Remember the parable in Mark 4, with Jesus and the disciples? Jesus had been preaching all day by the lake. The crowds were so large that He actually got in a boat and drifted on the lake while he shared parables (stories). Picture the scene in your mind: large crowds of people pushing in ever-so closely to the very edge of the lake; not even a whisper was heard because each longed to hear every word the teacher spoke.

This is one of my favorite Bible stories because I can picture it like a movie in my mind: Jesus in the boat, on a calm lake, drifting slowly with only the smallest ripples from His weight within the boat, with the glimmer of sun rays going down behind Him. Can you see it? I imagine the setting is so peaceful. As the boat moved downstream, the crowds continued to move ever-so slightly in the direction of His voice. Then in Mark 4:35–41, evening came and Jesus said to His disciples, "Let us go over to the other side." Leaving the crowd behind, it was now just the disciples and Jesus.

On the lake that night, a furious wind came up, and the boat was swaying, dipping violently up and down with each crashing wave causing the boat to take on water. The disciples couldn't believe it . . . Jesus was sleeping! They were whining and complaining among themselves and to themselves. Can't you just imagine their thoughts? *How can He sleep through this storm? Hey, Jesus! We could use some help here!* The disciples were in a panic when they finally decided to wake Jesus up, and they said to Him, "Teacher, don't You care if we drown?" Jesus simply got up, rebuked the wind, and said to the waves, "Quiet! Be still!" Then the wind died down and it was completely calm. Then He asked His disciples, "Why are you so afraid? Do you still have no faith?"

The disciples lived with Jesus. They walked with Him and ate with Him, laughed with Him, and experienced life with Him. How disappointing that they still didn't believe 100 percent that Jesus was the Messiah. They asked each other, "Who is this? Even the wind and the waves obey Him!"

Sometimes, like the disciples, we too need to be reminded that God calms the storms in our life. We can worry and have anxiety, causing fear and sleepless nights. We can wonder, *Where is Jesus? Does He really care? Is He who He says He is?* Or we can have faith and trust that He will do as He said He will do because He is who He says He is. If God has the power in His voice to calm the sea, He has the power in His voice to calm the storms in your life.

Those are wonderful promises to hold onto and to trust, but once again, can you imagine the disappointment the human side of Jesus felt when those who knew Him best still didn't believe? What an example that life will have its disappointments. Yes, even Church Ladies will go through storms in this life.

Robin's life was in the midst of a storm that night. The girls' night out was our lake, our time to get away, just Jesus and us. We needed to hear the stories of those who we love, so we could be used by God to love, to hug, to encourage, and to be a voice to a hurting sister.

Sometimes, even those who have an intimate relationship with Jesus Christ need to express their feelings and emotions outwardly. However, please know that I am not promoting complaining and arguing, or gossip or negative thinking — or whining, for that matter. Not at all. It is true that whiners are self-absorbed and annoying! In fact, if you've heard it once, you've heard it a thousand times: no whining allowed!

However, after my girls' night out, it just seemed like an appropriate and fun play on words to title this chapter "The Whine Club." And it's so true that all Church Ladies need to whine every once in a while. We're ladies! We're real people with real hurts, real struggles, and real needs. The longing to express what is on our hearts may sometimes come out as whining; however, most of the time it's simply a form of getting it out, to keep Satan from keeping it in.

The Whine Club is when two or more get together and share life's ups and downs; a time to talk about the genuine cares, heartbreaks, children, hot topics, and celebrations — let's just say concerns of the Church Lady. Sometimes those concerns may feel gigantic like the giant Goliath coming toward you, where fear and worry seem to choke the life out of you. And other times, it may be a little thing; however, it seems to nag at you and consume your thoughts. Just remember, no matter what, it's big to the one who needs to share. And our God is big enough to handle it!

TIPS TO CONSIDER BEFORE YOU WHINE

- Pray! Take everything to the Lord in prayer. Seek Him first!
- Only whine in a safe place.
- Proverbs 18:7: The mouths of fools are their ruin; their lips get them into trouble.
- Proverbs 20:6: Many will say they are *loyal friends*, but who can find one that is really *faithful?*
- Proverbs 21:21: Whoever pursues godliness and unfailing love will find life, godliness, and honor.
- Sometimes we should refrain from whining when we feel the need, and be quiet! The Holy Spirit lives *in us* to *guide* and *protect us*. If you are in a conversation and you hear this voice, find a way out. The Holy Spirit is here to protect us.
- Proverbs 21:23: If you *keep your mouth shut,* you will stay out of trouble.
- Proverbs 21:29: The wicked put up a bold front but the upright *proceed with care.*

There are times when you are told something in confidence. Now that you have this information, be responsible, be a trustworthy friend — in other words, don't repeat it!

Do everything without grumbling or arguing, so that you may become blameless and pure, children of God without fault in a warped and crooked generation. Then you will shine among them like stars in the sky as you hold firmly to the word of life. (Philippians 2:14–16)

THE WHINE CLUB

To be in this club, you must:

- Be a Church Lady with godly ambition.
- Be a true friend who props others back up, dusts them off, and encourages them that tomorrow is a new day.
- Love Jesus and desire to live your life reflecting Him.
- Genuinely love, support, and nurture others in the club.
- Be a good listener. Be trustworthy!
- Admit you are not perfect, therefore you too need friends in the Whine Club.
- Not allow negative thoughts to take up root in your heart. You instead quickly pull out the bad seed and plant something positive. You want to encourage others like Paul does. Read Philippians 4:6–9.
- Put Jesus first, others second, and yourself third.

Every Church Lady (that means you) is invited to be in the club.

SOMEBODY, HELP ME!

How many times have you wished someone could just "fix it"? (Texan for "make it right.") As Christians, we need friends, but what we really need is an intimate relationship with Jesus. When we come to our *wits' end* and desperation *sets in,* Jesus is the only one who can truly "fix it." His ways are not our ways. *"Many are the plans in a person's heart, but it is the Lord's purpose that prevails"* (Proverbs 19:21).

On my journey I have had the privilege to speak with many people — men, women, and students — who have experienced pain and suffering, grief and mourning, illness and addiction. Each one has given great testimony that, after making it through the storm, they wouldn't change a thing. Although the suffering is unbearable at times, and the loss of a loved one made them ask the Lord to take them home too, or the weight of the debt owed seemed too heavy to carry, they now see how the Lord used this painful time as a growing time and, in the end, for good in their life. Each story I hear seems to have the same ending: "All glory to God!"

The One who created us is the One who knows best for us. Whether a storm is approaching, or you have just come through the storm of all storms, it is essential to keep your focus on Him, not on the problem, the person who has hurt you, the child who has disappointed you, or the friend who has let you down. But instead recognize it is in the storms of life where God has your undivided attention. It is in times of desperation you become desperate for God to help you.

Looking back over your life, can you see how during the storms was when you became closer to God? Can you see that spiritual growth was greater in these times of desperation, when you were helpless, dependent on Him alone? When nothing or no one could say or do the right thing, so out of desperation, you turned to Him? Do you believe that God has a purpose and a plan for your life? Do you believe that God will use you to bring Himself glory? Can you give testimony that when you are weak, He is strong? Can you see how in times of suffering you have become closer, perhaps more intimate with God than before? And wouldn't you agree that in these times you wouldn't want to be anywhere else but in the loving arms of Jesus? You see, in the end, God receives all the glory!

Now if we are children, then we are heirs — heirs of God and co-heirs with Christ, if indeed we share in his sufferings in order that we may also share in his glory. (Romans 8:17, NLT)

*P*RAYER

Dear God, You get the glory for this one too!
Period. The end. Amen.

REVEAL AND TRANSFORM

1. Pray. Ask the Lord to help you be sensitive the next time another Church Lady needs to whine.

2. How do you relate to the problems of others? Do you really listen?

3. When was the last time you needed to share a worry or concern with a friend? Did she listen? What was her response? Was it helpful?

4. When was the last time you remember a problem or concern consuming your thoughts? Can you see how your problems can take the focus off God and put it on *me*? Share your thoughts.

5. Is there something you've been keeping in and you are about to burst to share? What is it?

6. Jesus used parables because they help listeners to discover truth about them. And the Bible either encourages or convicts the heart of the one who reads it. *Church Lady* is full of stories of women like you. Prayerfully God will use these real stories to make a positive impact on your life. Have you gained any insight, been encouraged, or been challenged? Explain.

7. Who is your whine club, the one or few that you can trust completely?
   Are you mostly the one sharing or are you a good listener too? God gives us opportunity to help and be there for others. How do you respond when a friend is troubled or has a crisis in her life? Remember, whether or not you think it's a crisis, it is to her.

8. Read this verse out loud:

Do everything without grumbling or arguing, so that you may become blameless and pure, children of God without fault in a warped and crooked generation. Then you will shine among them like stars in the sky as you hold firmly to the word of life. (Philippians 2:14–16)

Your thoughts?

9. We should take our cares and concerns to God in prayer first. There are times when we need to discuss it only upward to the Lord. If we wait, if we are still, He will answer us.

Many are the plans in a person's heart, but it is the Lord's purpose that prevails. (Proverbs 21:30)

Can you recall the last time you shared something but wish you would have waited? I call this *getting ahead of God*. Share about a time when you prayed, you cried out to Jesus, and you waited on Him . . . and He answered you.

10. When was the last time you were grateful for a friend who simply listened and/or gave godly advice?

Pray.

Church Lady Surprise

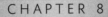

When God's people are in need, be ready to help them.
Always be eager to practice hospitality.

— ROMANS 12:13 (NLT)

ave you ever enjoyed eating a meal but you had no idea what the ingredients were? Perhaps it looked like the cook had opened every can in her pantry to prepare this meal. You can't figure it out, but it's oh-so tasty! I think the Lord does this in our lives with people. He throws some of this and some of that in the mix to spice things up.

For years I enjoyed lunch with my girlfriends at least two times a month. Phone visits were almost every day. Then, like rain showers in the desert, my time with friends became few and far between. Planning date nights with other couples on the weekends seemed to be a thing of the past, and finding myself on the road again or in the air again meant one thing: another lonely weekend.

Keeping my priorities in order were a must if I wanted my marriage to stay strong, to be the best mom I could be, and be a student of God's Word so I'd be ready for God to use me at any given moment. This meant time with friends fell to fourth or fifth place on the list. And who has time for more than one through three in any given week?

A friend had given me a book to read that said setting boundaries is a must for people in ministry, so I said no to lunch dates with friends, shopping days, and spur-of-the-moment invitations. In the beginning I thought for sure it was a sacrifice that God had asked me to make, and this is how my road to loneliness began.

MY DISTRESS CALL TO GOD

After two years I cried out to the Lord, "Father God, I didn't know this ministry vocation would mean I had to give up my friends. Am I doing something wrong here? You know I'm a people person, Lord (like He needed to be reminded), and I've had enough time with me, myself, and I. Lord, I miss my friends! Show me, Lord! What do I need to change?" My ever-so patient heavenly Father was shaking His head at such a silly request, I was sure. But I wanted to at least make my request. *Ask and you shall receive* (Matthew 7:7).

Soon I could see how He took me under His merciful wings and gently began to remove the blinders *I* had tacked on so tightly to the side of my eyes. Remember, *I* had put up the blinders to help *me* focus on *my* priority list. While trying my best to do the right thing, it seemed my heart and my mind were playing a game of tug of war and those blinders began to have a negative impact in my life.

Jeremiah prayed, "I know, Lord, that our lives are not our own. We are not able to plan our own course. So correct me, Lord, but please be gentle. Do not correct me in anger, for I would die." (Jeremiah 10:23–24, NLT).

Lonely and unhappy, I had come to a place of desperation, or maybe I was depressed and didn't know what to call it. Maybe you too have experienced times of desperation in your life, a place where you were humbled and demonstrated no resistance to discipline or a new idea. You beg the Father to speak and give wisdom and direction, to help you climb out of this deep and dark hole you've fallen into.

THE DREAM

After a few months in this lowly place, the Lord began to show me that I had put this heavy yoke upon myself. In the stillness one night I had a dream. I saw a hard-shelled box that I had put myself in for protection. Satan quickly shut the lid and began to use the box for his footstool. In the dream I could see Satan smiling as he perched his big, heavy, ugly feet on the box, keeping the lid tightly pressed down. In desperation I called out to God and immediately He pushed Satan's feet from the box and removed the lid. When I saw the Lord, I reached my hands up as high as I could. In that moment the Father reached down and with one gentle tug He pulled me out. He then literally removed the blinders from my eyes. He bathed me in his mercy and for the first time in a long time I could see clearly and *all* around me. As the Lord carried me in His loving arms I felt such freedom, and I knew He had more in store for my life than I could ever hope for or imagine (Ephesians 3:20). Then the Lord took me to a large body of water and placed my feet on this huge wave. I stood upright in faith and began to ride on His wave of goodness and mercy! It was awesome!

FLASHBACK

At 16 years old during a summer youth camp, God put a calling on my heart and I knew that full-time ministry would be my vocation. Confident that God would do the work through me, there were still many unanswered questions. I knew the who (me) and the what (working for the Lord); however, the when, where, and how were still a big question. My pastor at that time said, "Chandra, step by step. He will be faithful to show you the way." And He has.

At the age of 19, I began to volunteer in student ministry. At 32, God opened a door for me to be the associate youth minister at a church in San Antonio, Texas. After serving there for five years, I believed in my heart that "this was it!" I loved student ministry and I became passionate about teaching God's truth to teenagers. Then one ordinary day, while driving from San Antonio to Houston, God spoke clearly to me. He said for me to resign my student ministry position and begin Godly and Beautiful (GAB) Ministry where He would open the doors for me to speak His Truth. Sure it was the Lord, I took a giant step of faith, resigned the following week, and He has been faithful every step of the way.

Perhaps you have not heard the voice of the Lord in such a personal manner and you are wondering how I have. Let me encourage you to develop an attitude of listening. I certainly do not have the answer, but I have my personal story. I am confident when we seek God, He answers. Each time the Lord has spoken to me (not audibly, but in Spirit) I have been seeking Him and praising Him without distraction. This time, I happened to be in my car. In the stillness is when He speaks to me.

In those early days of my ministry, it was common for me to stay with church members when I was speaking at events. Although I enjoyed the fellowship, there were some awkward moments.

Once, while I was staying with a minister of youth and his sweet wife after speaking to their youth, upon my arrival they took me to the room where I would sleep. "How cute!" I raved as this young mommy opened the door.

"This is little Johnny's room, but tonight he is going to give it to you."

I smiled as I looked around the room of their three-year-old. The theme was clearly choo-choo trains, as they adorned the walls and the sheets on which I would sleep. After the event, tired and ready for some rest, I nestled into the twin-size bed. I don't remember going to sleep; however, I do remember waking up suddenly at 3:30 A.M. to a little boy climbing into *his* bed with me. He snuggled up close and I'm not sure he ever realized I wasn't his mommy. As you can imagine, I didn't get much sleep that night. I didn't know whether to get up and go to the couch, to wake the parents up, or what. So, I laid there awake, praying that no one would ever use this against me. I could see the headline — "Female minister sleeps with little boy." Early Sunday morning, his parents begin to look for him. Since I had been awake for hours, I was glad to hear them stirring. "He's in here," I pointed as I quietly opened the door. Of course, he was sound asleep, comfy in his bed. We had a good laugh, to say the least, and the news traveled quickly through the halls of their church that Sunday morning.

Another funny experience: I would be staying at this particular house for three nights while I spoke in public high schools on sexual abstinence in this particular community. When the sweet Church Lady (who was so pleased to have me staying with her) showed me to my room and also to the bathroom that I would be sharing with her teenage son...do I need to say more?

While in Mississippi, the church had me stay with an elderly lady who lived alone and was the epitome of the Church Lady. She graciously welcomed me into her home (decorated with lace doilies, collectibles, and family photos) as I followed her to the kitchen where she had made three casserole dishes the week before and had put them in the freezer. She explained that she would pull them out and pop them into the oven an hour before I came home each evening. The bad news: she had three cats and I am highly allergic. On Friday morning when I woke up, I could hardly breathe, my eyes were red, and I sneezed at least once every 5 minutes. They called the local pharmacist, who was also a deacon at the church. Within 15 minutes Benadryl (non-drowsy) was delivered to her door. We postponed the first session until after lunch while the event leaders took me to a new host home. So sad!

This one wins the prize! I was once again staying with a newly married minister of youth and his wife, when in the middle of the night I heard some — let's just say *private* — things that I didn't need to hear. The rest of the weekend, I could not get those noises out of my head. Every time that I mentioned "save sex for marriage," I wanted to laugh out loud knowing this young couple was enjoying it in theirs.

Needless to say, there came a point in my ministry where guidelines would be given. One of those guidelines: hotel lodging. From that time on, I stayed in hotels and never had to worry about having a good night of rest, walking in on someone, or someone walking in on me. Who knew that this request would also be the door that led me down the road to loneliness?

Looking back, I know now that God taught me so much about people and ministry during those early days. Those experiences kept me humble, and after all, that had been my prayer from the beginning and is still my prayer today.

FLASH-FORWARD AGAIN: EXPECT THE UNEXPECTED!

Once the blinders were off my eyes, God took me from lonely hotel room weekends of ministry to the homes of Church Ladies who would minister to me. It seemed there was no limit to His provision. When I walked into the homes of these Church Ladies, it was a sweet, unexpected gift from God. The warmth, the fragrance, the fellowship — like melted butter dripping off a large homemade cinnamon roll just out of the oven. It was wonderful!

The very next weekend (after the vision) I would be traveling to a small Texas town. When I arrived the minister of youth said that I would be staying with a sweet elderly couple, Mr. and Mrs. Chapel. I couldn't believe it!

My daddy — who had gone to be with the Lord two years earlier — on that very same date had helped me pick out a Thomas Kinkade painting that was extremely special to me, called *The Forest Chapel*. Oddly enough, I felt the Lord used the Chapels to remind me He is in control of every detail, and it comforted me. And I don't believe in coincidences.

It was late when I arrived on their doorstep, around 11:00 p.m. Weather delay made me late. They had graciously waited up for me and welcomed me with open arms. My bed was turned down, they made sure I had something to drink, and already had my alarm set for the correct time.

After speaking to students the next day, I arrived at their front door at 9:30 in the evening. Mrs. Chapel had a small snack ready for me and we had a nice visit while I ate. Then before I went to bed, she and Mr. Chapel gave me a book, *The Purpose-Driven Life* by Rick Warren. This was very significant because while I was traveling to other churches sharing the good news, my home church was going through this study. Just another thing I was missing out on. They prayed with me before I went to bed. He prayed for my family and my ministry; she prayed for my rest and that I would be refreshed to speak to their students the following day. I could not hold back the tears as we hugged. The warmth, the touch, the prayer, it had to be God in them that knew exactly what I needed. Thanking them for their wonderful hospitality, I went up the stairs to bed. In a way, I felt like a child that had been tucked in to bed. Peaceful. Safe. Loved.

About three weeks later I was going to Midland, Texas, where I would be staying with Lisa. She had invited me to stay in her home, where the high school girls Bible study group had been working through one of my Bible studies. She picked me up from the airport, and the first thing she said was, "How would you like a spa treatment? Everyone likes to be pampered and this is my gift to you. Is that OK?" With a huge grin on my face, I said, "Of course. How sweet of you!" I couldn't believe it! What an unexpected gift. During that weekend, it felt like I was staying with one of my girlfriends. Precious!

The very next weekend I had an event in Edmonton, Oklahoma, where again I would be staying in a home. Boy, once I put the Lord back in charge it was obvious that He had a plan! Mr. and Mrs. Nelson greeted me with a hug. They said they were so excited to have me in their home and that they had prayed for me since the day they found out I would be staying with them. (It had been a couple of months ago that I booked the event.) Then they gave me a choice of rooms. Mrs. Nelson (which again was special because that is my maiden name) shared that while her husband's calling is marriage counseling, hers is hospitality. "It is my joy to serve others. We have had ministers, missionaries, and couples stay here, all that need a getaway. With grown children and rooms to spare, we turned our home into a 'ministry' bed and breakfast." As she was telling me this, we were walking down the hall as she showed me the beautiful rooms, each one very different: The Victorian Suite, lacy and girly; The Lodge, green and red plaid bedding, a log wall, etc. "With these two rooms inside and a little cottage outside, you can take your pick." She smiled. I was so excited and so indecisive! She suggested that I stay in a different room each night. Wow! Each evening when I came home, my things were in a different room. She asked what time I wanted to wake up each morning and what time I wanted breakfast served. You would not believe the breakfast this Church Lady prepared for me — strawberry crepes, fruit, waffles, eggs, bacon, orange juice, and chocolate milk. It was delicious! I didn't want to leave! The last night of my visit, she made dinner and the three of us ate together at their kitchen table. After dinner they prayed for my marriage, my ministry, and my walk with the Lord. We talked about ministry and life. Before I went out to my cottage, I shared with them how God had truly used them to bless me.

As I lay in bed that night, I thanked God for Mrs. Nelson and the other sweet Church Ladies who had touched my life those past few weeks. I couldn't help but think that each experience was unique and just what I needed.

God changed my heart and my joy was running over. This experience taught me that there is no cookie cutter for the Church Lady, but there is a recipe: God's purpose mixed with our obedience and unique personality. Look different? Oh yes! From hairstyles, fashion, shoe preference, culture, personality, to her mood, she's different and always changing. But the One who created her, the One who called her to Himself, the One who gave her purpose, He is constant. He never changes. From those who lived centuries ago to the modern Church Ladies of our day, a relationship with Jesus Christ is the one thing required that gives us the privilege to be called the Church Lady.

Oh yes, you shaped me first inside, then out; you formed me in my mother's womb. I thank you, High God — you're breathtaking! [...] I worship in adoration — what a creation! You know me inside and out, You know every bone in my body; You know exactly how I was made, bit by bit, how I was sculpted from

*nothing into something. Like an open book, you watched me grow from concep-
tion to birth; all the stages of my life were spread out before you. The days of my
life all prepared before I'd even lived one day.* (Psalm 139:14–16 *The Message*)

God created us, made us unique and in His image. So it should come at
no surprise that when we serve others, it is not only a blessing to those we
serve, but we too are blessed! What a beautiful reflection of our Father.

LIVING OUT OF THE OVERFLOW

God's blessings have been many and it seems that I began a new season
of life, a life full of joy overflowing with blessings. It was different than
anything I had prayed for and so much more than I ever dreamed of.
I was simply requesting more time with my girlfriends –the fabulous six.
The Lord instead began to open my eyes to Church Ladies everywhere
I went. Before I knew it, I was seeing my friends more, which included
those special lunch dates.

It was clear that my efforts to protect myself had boxed me in. Only
God Himself, His power working through me, would keep everything
in order — the ministry, my marriage, family, and even my much-needed
"girl time," all in balance. He got my full attention during this dry, lonely
season. I have learned to rest in Him and wait on Him before making any
decisions. When we trust in Him alone, He will do the work and we will
live out of the overflow. Living in the overflow, there is no stress. And the
freedom we experience when we rely on Him, ah . . . the peace while riding that wave is priceless!

One year we had so much rain in our area that the dams on the lakes
were overflowing. There was nothing that anyone could do to stop the
overflow. The people downstream had to get out of the way and run
to safety. That's not the case when we experience overflow from what
God is doing in the Christian life. There is no hurried scramble and
stress to get out of the way. No. Instead, in the overflow is where we find
rest, peace, and calm. Riding this wave of overflow *is* the abundant life!
We don't miss out when we live in His overflow. Are you stressed about
something today? If so, give it to God. Rest in Him. Wait on Him and you
too will experience the peace that is birthed out of your nothingness and
His overflow. Learning this lesson has made all the difference in my life!

I stopped being so rigid and have become more fluid. It's wonderful! You should try it. I recognize that some of those spur-of-the-moment opportunities are the best ones. I'm not as hurried as I use to be; therefore, I notice what is going on around me.

While at the grocery store I saw a darling elderly lady on her tip-toes reaching for an ingredient located on the top shelf. I said, "Looks like you need some help. Let me get that for you."

"Oh honey, can you reach it? They put things so high up that you need to tote a stepstool with you to the grocery store these days." We laughed. She told me what she was baking that day and realized she didn't have any vanilla bean. She went on to tell me that she had always depended on her husband to reach things, but that he had passed away a year ago. We stood there and talked for at least 15 minutes and then I gave her a hug and told her that I would pray for her when I thought about her. "Honey, I sure do appreciate that. I don't have any family here other than my church family. What would I do without those Church Ladies?"

I couldn't believe it. Was she an angel that God had placed there to encourage me? Or perhaps He wanted to see if I would take time out of my busy day to speak to this lonely lady. Thankfully I had. As she spoke, something inside told me that she was just lonely and needed someone to listen. My heart was grateful and I knew that if God had not allowed me to go through my season of loneliness, I might have been too busy to stop and listen to her. And the fact that she said *Church Lady* made me smile as I walked away. I knew then that God would have me include her in this chapter.

This humble servant has tasted His mercy once more and I am forever grateful for each Church Lady who passes through my life.

*P*RAYER

Oh Lord, don't let me get so busy that I run ahead of You. I want to be in Your will; but when I am not, quickly correct me and put me back where You want me to be . . . in step with you. Amen.

I'm so thankful that the Lord corrected me gently. He opened my eyes and helped me to see that we put restraints on ourselves, therefore creating needless worry, pain, and suffering in our lives. Without recognizing it, perhaps you too have put yourself in the driver's seat. If so, give Him back His rightful place today.

Now that I have experienced doing life this way, I don't ever want to go back. Daily I pray that He will make whatever is wrong in my life right, and that He will keep me on course for His plan.

The Lord continues to bless me by putting Church Ladies in my path. Since I've begun riding this wave, I've come to expect the unexpected! It's fun! It's exciting! And I'm always waiting for the next Church Lady surprise.

God has opened the doors for me to travel with World Hope Ministry to Africa two times. Believing in this ministry and that God wants me to continue to partner with World Hope Ministry, I was looking forward to attending a World Hope fundraiser. Much to my surprise, my family and I were seated at the table with the founder, Dr. Harold Davis. Although I had personally never met Dr. Davis, I had heard a lot about him from his son Dwight Davis, vice-president of the ministry and also the missions pastor at my church.

Africa is a democracy in turmoil, a continent tattered and torn, a people hungry and empty. World Hope feeds these people food to satisfy their hunger, and spiritual food found in the hope of Jesus Christ. My life will never be the same after seeing this firsthand. So for me to get to meet Dr. Davis was a thrill and a privilege. To express my gratitude to him personally was priceless.

I visited with this still-vibrant elderly man whose love for Jesus is emphatic! After sharing stories about World Hope and what we have seen the Lord do there, Dr. Davis wanted to know more about my ministry. We talked until the program began and then I hesitantly returned to my seat which was across the round table from him. At the close of the evening, the woman sitting beside me leaned over my shoulder and asked if I had a business card. She introduced herself as Carolyn, Harold's (Dr. Davis's) sister. She then shared how she had always wanted to write a book and never had, but she was so excited to hear what my ministry was doing in the lives of students through my speaking and the Bible studies I had written. One thing led to another, and she asked if I was working on anything at this time. When I shared with her that I was writing *Church*

Lady, she was thrilled! In that moment the Holy Spirit impressed on me to ask her to pray for me because I desperately needed a quiet place to write. She looked at my card and said that I might be hearing from her in a few days. With that said, the night was over and we both expressed how we knew it was divine intervention that we sat at the same table.

As I write this, it has been two weeks since I met Carolyn. I am sitting at a dark wood dining table covered with Bibles and papers in a beautiful lake home owned by Dr. Harold Davis. In front of me are ten huge panels of glass, a beautiful lake, green pastures on the other side, and I am ever-so reminded that God provides all that we need, and that He is full of surprises when we ride on the overflow of His mercy and grace. God, You are awesome! I love You and thank You for showing me Your reflection in the lives of Church Ladies along my journey.

There have been times when I thought, *Oh no, maybe this wave is coming to an end.* Then God reminds me through His Word that He will keep in perfect peace all who trust in Him, whose thoughts are fixed on Him!

When my eyes are fixed on Him, what I see is amazing! And not if, but when this wave I'm enjoying crashes onto dry land, I'm confident that He will be right there to pick me up, clean me off, and teach me yet another lesson in life. And just like today, my heart will be glad and full of praise and adoration to Him.

REVEAL AND TRANSFORM

1. When you consider those who have walked this journey with you, it is fun to also consider those who simply crossed your path and made a lasting impact on your life. Who are these people in your life?

2. Looking back, have you ever put up unnecessary boundaries that perhaps kept you from joy or opportunity?

3. Read Jeremiah 10:23. Have you tried to plan your own course? When did you realize you needed to let go and let God?

4. Who has the Lord used to help you escape a desperate time in life?

5. The Lord was making Himself known in every detail of my life. How has He reminded you that He is in control?

6. In what areas are you gifted in regards to hosting? Remember, not everyone has the gift of hosting like Mrs. Nelson, but we can all invite others into our home.

7. When guests enter your home, what is the most important thing you want them to feel or recognize? How can you assure they will?

8. What makes you unique? (Psalm 139:14–15)

9. In the season of riding the wave, you are in a season of freedom, totally dependent on the Lord. Are you on the wave?

10. Have you boxed yourself in? Kick the lid off, sister, and let God be in charge. His way is so much better than ours. Write your thoughts.

CHAPTER 9

The Giant

Bless those who persecute you.
Don't curse them; pray that God will bless them.

— ROMANS 12:14 (NLT)

"Miss Peele! Miss Peele!" the third-grade girl called out as she waved her hand in the air. It was the first day of school and the end of the day. Miss Peele (my daughter) was scrambling to assure no child was left behind: "Bus riders in this line. Car riders in this one. Afterschool care over here, please."

"Miss Peele. Miss Peele!" Finally the determined little girl got her attention amidst all the chaos.

"Yes," said Miss Peele.

"Are you Bap-i-tist or Cath-o-lic?" (written as she said it) asked the little girl.

Miss Peele smiled, put her arm around the little girl, and said, "I just love Jesus!"

What a sweet reminder that being a reflection of Jesus is the most important lesson Miss Peele will ever teach. After all, Jesus too wants to assure no child is left behind.

Although most Church Ladies may never face severe persecution, rest assured Satan has a strategy to bring us affliction, to keep us from the will of God. In spite of the rule *check your faith at the door* in public school, the love of Christ cannot be contained. His love, power, and truth will flow from our heart into our words and actions. In fact, being told not to share our faith goes against everything Jesus teaches. How can a Christ follower hide her or his love for God when His power dwells within them? Isn't being asked not to share our faith a form of persecution? Too bad not everyone who recognizes Christ in us will be as excited as the little girl.

Jesus said, "Let the little children come to me, and do not hinder them, for the kingdom of heaven belongs to such as these" (Matthew 19:14). He instructs us to "love the Lord with all your heart and with all your soul and with all your mind; [and] love your neighbor as yourself" (Matthew 22:37, 39).

The Bible is full of stories that give examples of those who have been persecuted because of their faith. Have you read 1 Samuel lately? If not, perhaps you should. Allow me to give you the short version of the story.

The Israelites had been at war with the Philistines for years. This war was much more than physical; it was a spiritual battle that still continues today. King Saul, Israel's first appointed king, was a good leader, but he became impatient and took matters into his own hands. He became arrogant and disobeyed God. In 1 Samuel 15, the Lord told Saul to destroy all the Amalekites and their livestock, sparing nothing. The Amalekites were evil people. Knowing the Amalekites would continue to destroy the Israelites, God ordered Saul to get rid of them and *everything* that was theirs. Instead Saul spared their king and their best livestock. It was apparent that Saul cared more about what the people thought and less about his relationship with God. God had entrusted Saul and he did not act responsibly.

I shake my head in disbelief every time I read how Saul deliberately disobeyed God. Did he really think he could get away with it? But then the Holy Spirit reminds me of my own disobedience. Yes, Saul was the king of Israel, and I'm just a Church Lady in the suburbs, but God desires all His children to have a pure heart, character, and integrity that reflect Him.

THE LORD REJECTS SAUL AS KING

Saul pleads for forgiveness but God rejects him as king. The Lord told Samuel to go to Bethlehem and find a man named Jesse, for he had selected one of his sons to be the new king of Israel (1 Samuel 16:1). When Samuel arrived, he took one look at Eliab, son of Jesse, and thought, *Surely this is the Lord's anointed!* Why? Because Eliab was tall, strong, and handsome as was Saul. But the Lord said to Samuel, "Do not consider his appearance or height, for I have rejected him. The Lord does not look at the things people look at. People look at the outward appearance, but the Lord looks at the heart" (v. 7)

Church Lady, did you hear that? While everything around us screams for us to have a certain look, be this weight, wear a particular brand of clothing, to live in a particular neighborhood, drive this kind of vehicle, and so on, God simply says, "I see your *heart*." I don't know about you, but this makes me want to step back and take a closer look at my heart.

Satan enjoys our negative self-talk. Like a giant, these thoughts hold us captive. They keep the focus on self instead of God, from being a blessing and/or receiving one. Perhaps we should spend more time in the Word, prayer, and serving others to assure our heart is right with the Lord, instead of spending needless time assuring we look good on the outside. (Ouch! Could the Lord be speaking to me?) This, sweet sister, is a giant many of God's daughters battle every day. And where is the battle fought? On the battlefield of our heart.

Satan, the ruler of the world, lures us with worldliness and temporary pleasures. He's crafty and wants us to believe truth is relative. Ultimately it's all about us, what *we* think, and what *we* want. His opponent — God the King of the world, the creator of all things — His love is unconditional and everlasting. He pursues us to focus on righteousness. His love and forgiveness are everlasting. His grace refines us for a purpose. He is Truth. He is always victorious!

When I was young, my brother would sit on me and hold me down. I could kick and try my best to move, but he knew I could never have the strength to win. As soon as I screamed for Mom or Dad to rescue me, he would get off. Satan does the same thing to us. He holds us captive until we cry out to our heavenly Father. And just hearing the name of Jesus, he runs.

Do you have any giants sitting on you, restraining you from going about the will of God? Call out to Jesus, lift up your hand, and ask the Lord to rescue you from your giants today.

GOD IS STRONGER!

Don't allow thoughts like *I'm divorced* and *Oh no! God hates divorce, I had an affair, I had an abortion, I had sex before I was married, I'm in debt, I'm a recovering alcoholic, I'm weak, I, I, I,* keep you from the will of God. Your negative thoughts, according to your flesh and man's opinion, is one of Satan's favorite battles to fight. Don't allow the giants of past sin, guilt, and insecurity hold you down a second longer. Call out to your heavenly Father. His power is greater! His love unconditional! It's not like picking the petals off a daisy. He loves you, girl! Forever and always! Embrace your freedom in Christ. Rise up in power and in strength.

Write these words on a sticky note and put it where you can see them: *I am a child of God. Jesus died once for my sin. Because of His great love for me, I am forgiven and free.* God has already won the battle, sister! His victory is ours! And don't forget the *I am beautiful* sticky note.

HANDPICKED BY GOD

David's story is good to consider when we struggle with the *I'm not good enoughs* or when we allow the thoughts and the opinions of others hold us back. David was *just a shepherd boy*. At least that's what his brothers thought. But God had a plan. He told Samuel to anoint David with oil because he was *the one* (1 Samuel 16:12). From that day forward, the Spirit of the Lord came upon David in power.

In the meantime, the Spirit of the Lord had departed from King Saul and he was tormented with an evil spirit. When the suggestion was made that perhaps music would calm him, one of Saul's servants recommended David. Coincidence? I don't think so. Every detail had been laid out according to God's plan. David went from playing the harp in the fields to playing in the palace, overnight. God sets our path. We simply need to follow Him.

NAYSAYERS

Don't listen to the words of the naysayers who say, "Oh, you're just a *shepherd boy*, you can't do that!" If David had taken those words to heart, there may not be a 1 Samuel in the Bible to read. On a personal note, if I had listened to those who said I wasn't qualified to speak or write, you certainly wouldn't be reading this book right now. The fact is that I know I can't, as did David, but I trust His power in me can!

When was the last time someone discouraged you? Did you give up? It's not too late. Pray, seek God; perhaps He will give you the desire again. Faith and obedience is the key. So if you are willing and obedient, hang on, Church Lady. Get ready for God to move you. And when you take that first step of faith, you'll know He's gotcha! It's a perk of being the daughter of the King.

DAVID AND GOLIATH

Churched or unchurched, almost everyone knows the story of David and Goliath (1 Samuel 17). The Israelites and the Philistines were at war. When the Israelites saw the giant, they ran from him in great fear. When David saw this he was in disbelief! *Are you seriously going to let this bully continue to play cat and mouse with you?* He couldn't believe that the army and his own brothers had allowed this to go on for 40 days! Curious, David began asking a lot of questions. When his brothers heard him, they were angry. They belittled him, told him to go back to his fields and take care of his few sheep. When brought before Saul, David said,

> *"Let no one lose heart on account of this Philistine; your servant will go and fight him." Saul replied, "You are not able to go out against this Philistine and fight him; you are only a young man, and he has been a warrior from his youth"* (vv. 32–33).

David's response was honorable:

> *"'Because this Philistine has defied the armies of the living God, I will do the same to him.' [With confidence he announced,] 'I have done this to both lions and bears, and I'll do it to this pagan Philistine, too, for he has defied the armies of the living God! The Lord who rescued me from the claws of the lion and the bear will rescue me from this Philistine!'"* (vv. 36–37 NLT).

Saul not only gave David his blessing to fight the Philistine, he gave David his personal armor: a tunic and coat of armor (as if wearing the king's garments could somehow protect him). After belting on his sword, David could hardly walk because the armor was so heavy. David took it off. He held his staff in one hand, picked up five smooth stones from the stream, put them in the pouch of his shepherd's bag, and with his sling in the other hand, he approached the giant.

After a few harsh words spoken by Goliath, David said, "You come against me with your sword and spear and javelin, but I come against you in the name of the Lord Almighty, the God of the armies of Israel, whom you have defied" (v. 45).

David ran (fearless) to the battle line to meet Goliath and, taking out a stone, he slung it and struck the Philistine on the forehead, and he fell facedown on the ground. When the Philistines saw their hero was dead, they turned and ran.

David had a different perspective than the troops. They were weak and indecisive and focused on the size of the giant. David saw a giant who defied his God. He had no fear. His faith was unwavering. David knew the power of God in him would defeat the giant. The question is, do we? Are we confident? Do we really trust in His power?

Where is your shepherd field? The place where you spend the most time? What tools has God taught you to use? What natural gifts has He given you? When giants come against you, and they will, do you run the other way or face them head-on, confident that you are prepared and that God is fighting with you?

WHO OR WHAT IS YOUR GIANT?

Since Lindsey was six years old she dreamed of being a teacher. She's a kid magnet, no doubt, and we've always known she would be an excellent teacher. Unfortunately, most of her creative ideas are no longer allowed in the public school, and the students . . . let's just say she never dreamed teaching would be such a challenge.

Sadie, for example, her most problematic student, can be sweet as pie one minute and a raging bull the next. One day when Sadie was out of control, Lindsey called her mom. "I don't know what to do either, Miss Peele. I'm so sorry that she is acting like this in your class. I can't sleep at night for worrying about it. She acts the same way at home. I love my daughter, but I'm at a loss! I don't know what to do," she tearfully expressed. Instead of blurting out the critical words she had planned, the Holy Spirit filled Lindsey's mouth with love and compassion. She told the mom she would pray for her and together they would work to resolve this bad behavior.

After Lindsey opened the door to pray for Sadie's mom, she could sense the mom's relief. She said, "Oh Miss Peele, thank you! And I'm praying for you too!" The opposition created by the school's rule to push God aside was gone. With a new perspective, the mom shared more details about Sadie. Turns out, Sadie is fighting some giants of her own. Maybe distracting the class is her way of getting some much-needed love and attention. I have a feeling God's using Lindsey more than she'll ever know.

Praise God for teachers like Lindsey who may not be able to write a Bible verse on the smart board in front of the class, but reflects it through their heart. One way or another, God's love and His Word spills out — if not in our words, in our actions and in that genuine love God has poured into the heart of every Church Lady.

Lindsey's giant is a little third-grade girl named Sadie. Through the power of prayer, that little giant is becoming smaller every day!

IT'S ALL RELEVANT — I DON'T THINK SO!

We may not be fighting on a battlefield with arrows and swords, but if you listen, you'll hear the thunder of war. Satan's strategy is gaining strength, especially when it comes to moral issues. Being harassed or singled out by this giant is certainly persecution. Church Lady, ready yourself, the battle is upon us.

As a soldier of the Lord, I've been on the frontlines for years now, especially teaching His truth in the area of moral purity. I've spoken in schools, both Christian and public, and of course to parents and students in the church. While most people applaud the abstinence message, there have been times when I've gotten the wind knocked out of my sails.

While I have come to expect opposition in the secular setting, I was appalled when I came face-to-face with this particular giant in a church. While at a mother-daughter retreat where I had been invited to speak on God's plan for marriage, I was shocked when teens disagreed with the abstinence message. After all, I was teaching out of the Bible. First Corinthians 6:9–20 and 1 Thessalonians 4:1–8 were my texts, and both clearly warn us to flee from sexual immorality. Several girls (15 to 17 years old) wanted to argue with me in the middle of my talk. Thankfully it was a small group. Regardless, I was shocked! Much to my surprise, the two leaders in the group never spoke up.

In my hotel room I felt an evil presence. I called two of my prayer partners and Bruce to pray with me and for me. I had never experienced spiritual warfare to this degree. Outside my room (I was on the first floor), a group of men were barbecuing all night for a big party the next day. I heard nonstop foul language, loud laughing, and degrading comments about women like I'd never heard before. Finally around 4:30 in the morning, after calling out the name of Jesus and praying most of the night, I was worn out. At some point I fell asleep and my alarm went off at 7:00 A.M. I showered and dressed and was at the church by 8:30. My first session was with the moms and I was relieved not to start my day with *the girls*.

The tables were arranged in a U shape, and about 20 moms came. I prayed and then shared with the moms what happened the night before. After only a few moments, one of the moms raised her hand to speak. She was beautiful, well-dressed, and appeared to be a godly woman. I just knew she would come to my defense and tell me how sorry she was that I had experienced this with their group of girls. However, that is not what happened. She began by saying, "We have a problem here. We spoke with our girls and we are not in agreement with your teaching." My heart was beating so intensely and I thought surely there had been a misunderstanding. It seemed as though I was on trial as she spoke. Most of the women were nodding their heads in agreement with her while a few moms sat unresponsive. I was crying out on the inside, *"God, are You there? You need to help me because I feel like I'm getting beat up on Your behalf. I've spoken Your truth in love. Now what?"*

The mom went on to say they had taught their daughters it is OK to have sex as long as it is mutual. They felt I should have talked more about sex education and less about my spiritual beliefs. "These are real issues and we thought you were going to talk to our girls about birth control, not about heartache and spiritual consequences. Girls are getting pregnant because of people like you who only teach the abstinence message. I don't mean to be rude, but you are foolish if you think students are abstaining," she said.

Other moms were agreeing and I seriously thought I could feel Satan's arrows pierce my heart. I held it together and felt the Lord fill me up with boldness to stand firm on His Word — and I did.

Then suddenly God swooped in and rescued me when another mom spoke up. She told her personal story to the group. She had gotten pregnant when she was 16 and her daughter was attending the retreat and had been there the night before. She looked at me and said, "Chandra, I am sorry. My daughter did not stay here last night. She called me to pick her up because she was so embarrassed how the girls treated you. I for one believe the Bible, and that is what you teach. I applaud you for speaking truth in the lives of these girls and I believe many will be changed by your teaching. Although I would not trade my Amber for anything in the world, I would not wish teen pregnancy on anyone. Heart issues and consequences are exactly what these girls need to hear. Thank you for staying true to God's Word." She then got up and left.

There was one session left with the girls. I stepped into a room where I prayed, asking the Lord for clear direction. After only a few moments the Holy Spirit brought the words of 1 Peter 3:15 to me: "But in your hearts set apart Christ as Lord. Always be prepared to give an answer to everyone who asks you to give the reason for the hope that you have. But do this with gentleness and respect."

About that time, the pastor knocked on the door. We went out into the hall where another man was standing. He said, "I'm Pastor _____ and I want you to meet _____, my life partner." Yes. The pastor was living a gay lifestyle. I was immediately released by the Lord, but there was something I had to do before I left.

I asked the pastor to get everyone together. My flesh was weak and I wanted to run as fast as I could, but I made my way to the front of the chapel where the girls and their moms were seated.

"Girls, moms, Pastor. I know that you will not be surprised to hear I won't be staying for the last session. However, I do want you to know that all I have said has been from God's holy inspired Word and I believe it to be absolute truth. I believe that 'all Scripture is God-breathed and is useful for teaching, rebuking, correcting, and training in righteousness, so that the servant of God may be thoroughly equipped for every good work' (2 Timothy 3:16–17).

"My prayer is that I have not offended you but that God's truth has spoken to you regardless of what you think about me. One last thing before I go. The danger of relativism is that there is chaos, no absolutes, and this is what happened here this weekend. While you believe the Bible is relative, I believe it to be true and for everyone. I believe truth is a person. Jesus said, 'I am the way and the truth and the life' (John 14:6). I'll be praying for you."

With that, I gathered my things and the lady who invited me to speak walked me to her car. On the way to the airport she wiped tears from her face as we sat silently for the first five minutes. Finally I said, "I can't believe after hearing me speak before, you chose me to teach. I feel that I was set up."

She said, "I'm the staff nurse here but I attend another church. I have known for years that God has me here for a bigger purpose. Every year it's my job to bring in a speaker to teach sex education. After I heard your biblical message at a national youth ministers conference, I knew God wanted me to have you speak His truth into the lives of these girls. God has given me such a love for these people, but I know they practice religion here, not relationship. I'm sorry for the way this has ended, but for a moment I saw God's truth bring light into this church. I have no regrets. What happened here was God's plan, not mine."

Wow! Another Church Lady who reflects Jesus regardless of the rules. We cried together as our hearts broke for this corrupt so-called church. Oh sister, when the church waters down God's Word to fit worldly and immoral desires, when pastors teach the Bible is relative instead of absolute truth, and when church is considered a country club instead of a place of worship, chaos will be prevalent.

In Paul's last letter to Timothy, he says:

> *"Flee the evil desires of youth and pursue righteousness, faith, love and peace, along with those who call on the Lord out of a pure heart. Don't have anything to do with foolish and stupid arguments, because you know they produce quarrels. And the Lord's servant must not be quarrelsome but must be kind to everyone, able to teach, not resentful. Opponents must be gently instructed, in the hope that God will grant them repentance leading them to a knowledge of the truth, and that they will come to their senses and escape from the trap of the devil, who has taken them captive to do his will"* (2 Timothy 2:22–26).

I am sure of this: God will never call us to do something then leave us stranded. When He calls us, all He requires is obedience. In the same way, God will be with us when we face the giants of life. No giant is too big for our God.

Paul in his last letter to Timothy tells us that "everyone who wants to live a godly life in Christ Jesus will be persecuted, while evildoers and impostors will go from bad to worse, deceiving and being deceived (2 Timothy 3:12–13).

God is calling Church Ladies to take a stand, to face the giant(s) head-on, to be obedient and faithful followers of our Lord and Savior Jesus Christ. People will criticize us, single us out, call us names, and tell us we are foolish. They did that to David, and we see how that story ended.

The next time you are challenged concerning your faith, pray for and bless those who persecute you.

REVEAL AND TRANSFORM

What I learned:
- God is preparing you for something — you have a purpose.
- There will always be critical people. Some will be those closest to you.
- What seems impossible to man is possible with God.
- Consistent obedience builds character.
- God looks at your heart, not your size or hairstyle.
- How do you deal with persecution?
- God is stronger than your giant(s).
- David loved Saul in spite of his jealous spirit.
- Will we confront those who defy our God?

1. If people persecute you because you are a Christian, don't curse them; pray that God will bless them (Romans 12:14). Does anyone or any specific event come to mind? Has there been a time when you prayed for someone who was ugly to you, and you saw a change in them and perhaps in you? Explain.

2. When we consider the giants of our day, the dysfunctional family seems to be at the top of the list which includes rebellious children, no family time, affairs, divorce, disrespect, abuse, spiritual differences, and lack of intimacy. Other giants are cancer, caring for aging parents, debt, having a wedding called off ten days before the big day, father-in-law accused of molesting his granddaughter, teen pregnancy, and loss of job — those I heard just last week. And then there are more: awaiting test scores for SAT, college funding, endless worry, bad thoughts, past sin, struggle with pornography, hate my job, trying to meet my bosses' expectations, etc. Giants! Wow! Someone always seems to have a bigger giant, don't they? If you aren't fighting a battle today, stay alert because unfortunately tomorrow you might be staring one in the face.

What is your greatest challenge (giant) today, and how are you managing it?

3. Everyone who knew David thought he was just a shepherd boy. Never think you are just a stay-at-home mom, just a teacher, just a wife, just a _____, because you are God's daughter and He has a plan for your life. If you feel invisible or unappreciated, write out your feelings.

4. Unfortunately, most people who spot Jesus in us aren't as sweet as that little girl on Lindsey's first day of school. And while it's always a blessing to recognize another Church Lady in the midst of battling it out with your giant(s), Paul warns us that in the last days, godlessness will be very prevalent even among Christians (Romans 1:18). While you may not be persecuted, it is sometimes difficult to live out your Christian life. When and with whom?

5. It has become more common to hear our Christian values torn down and made fun of in the media. If you watch primetime TV, you will agree. What was socially unacceptable five years ago is accepted today. If you were born in the 1970s and earlier, your children and their children will grow up in a different culture than we have known. Christian values have been watered down to the point that unless one looks very close, it is not recognizable. What's right and wrong . . . most people don't care. What matters to them is how it makes them look and feel. *Indecisive*. Now there's a word worth talking about. In our faith how many times have you been indecisive about taking a stand for what is right? Or speaking out when something is wrong or against God's Word? Surrender to God and trust Him with the outcome.

6. Do you stand against those who defy your God? When have you and how did you take a stand?

7. Saul was Israel's first appointed king. He became arrogant, impatient, and he took matters into his own hands. He disobeyed God. He only ran to God after his own ideas had failed. When fighting your spiritual battles, do you push God aside, take matters into your own hands? Become impatient, try to resolve things your way, only to call on God as a last resort?

If someone were to watch you under pressure, what would they see? One who finds peace in the midst of turmoil? Who understands that spiritual character is built under pressure? Who trusts the Lord's plan? Or a fearful, stressed-out Church Lady who caves under pressure? I've been both. How about you?

8. I've talked to a lot of Church Ladies through the years and I'm amazed at how many giants there are! If these giants were a literal ball and chain, you too would be surprised to see all of the burdens Church Ladies carry around. Unfortunately, many of His daughters are being held captive by giants when He's given us the power to defeat them. No wonder our heavenly Father gave me this assignment. He'll do whatever it takes to get the attention of his girls, to help us discover the freedom to be who He has created us to be. We may be able to fool our friends and family and other Church Ladies too, but you can't fool God. Our heavenly Father knows everything about us. Things that are hidden or unspoken — He knows. He sees through all the cover-up. He sees your heart.

If your giant is something you did or went through in your past, let me encourage you. Do you believe that Jesus Christ paid your penalty and mine on a cross more than 2,000 years ago? Then let it go — God certainly has. How do I know? Because the Bible tells me so! In Romans 3:23–26, Paul gives us the good news. We have all sinned and are justified freely by His grace through the redemption that came through Christ Jesus. In other words, Jesus paid the debt for our sin so we don't have to keep looking back! We are free from those wrongs.

Praying you experience deliverance — freedom from bondage — today!

My Dad—The Church Man

Be happy with those who are happy,
And weep with those who weep.

— ROMANS 12:15 (NLT)

*I*t's Sunday morning. Dad's up early, and the aroma of coffee fills the house. Dressed in his slacks, collared shirt, and tie, he holds a cup of coffee in one hand and his Bible in the other. You can hear the Oral Roberts singers in the background as he looks over his Sunday School lesson one more time. "Breakfast!" Dad calls out. Rushing to the table, I pull my hair back into a half ponytail. "Morning, girls," he says, giving Melissa and me a kiss on the cheek. "Morning, son," he nods to my brother. As we take our places at the kitchen table, we bow our heads and Dad says the blessing — hot biscuits, gravy, and chocolate milk, or cinnamon toast was what I remember the most.

While putting his arms through one sleeve and then the next of his suit coat, Dad looks at his watch and reminds us not to forget our offering envelope and Bible. Then in a flash he is backing the station wagon out of the garage awaiting our arrival. Mom, in the meantime, is making a few last-minute preparations for Sunday dinner. After sliding the roast into the oven, she makes her way to the bathroom *one more time* and, as always, is the last one to the car.

Not every Sunday was this smooth, let me tell you. However, that was a typical Sunday morning at the Nelson home. Funny how those memories can be recalled quicker than pushing "rewind" on a DVR. The blessing of having had a godly dad is something I will never take for granted. However, as I write these words, there is a nudge in my spirit that says perhaps I shouldn't share this because not everyone had the same experience. Then my next thought is that *everyone* needs an example of what it's like to have a great dad. *A father to the fatherless, a defender of widows, is God in his holy dwelling* (Psalm 68:5).

Dad loved and respected his wife (Mom), provided for our family, and took care of our home. To him, these qualities were the measure of a godly man. Integrity and character were very important to Dad, therefore he was greatly respected by everyone who knew him. He believed that the man should be the spiritual leader of his home, and that he should also be a leader in his second family, the church. My dad was a church man. He loved people and there was never a doubt that God's Word was written on his heart because it was reflected in his lifestyle.

You might be wondering by now if my dad was real. Or perhaps you're wondering if I thought he was perfect. Absolutely not! Believe me, I could tell you some of those stories too, but . . . not today. Instead I want to honor him by sharing with you something he shared with me.

As God gave the vision for this book, He also put on my heart that *church men* play an enormous role in the life of the Church Lady. Think about the godly men who have passed through or perhaps still are a part of your journey. Those who have taught you about Jesus, who have touched your life, helped shape you into the Church Lady you are today. Can you name them? Pastors, teachers, fathers, uncles, friends, husbands, etc. Although I can count on two hands the godly men who have greatly impacted my life, my dad's influence towers above them all.

ABOUT MY DAD

My dad became a Christian at 11 years old, which was three years after his dad was killed in Germany while serving our country in World War II. Being the oldest of five children (at the time) and living on a farm, he had more responsibility than I can imagine. At 17, he felt the Lord's call on his life to be a pastor. He wanted to go to Baylor University, which would support his calling. Unfortunately, he was not aware that he could have received a scholarship from Baylor because of his hardship and good grades. Therefore, after graduation, instead of college, he signed up for the military.

In August 1956, Dad was drafted into the navy. The following Christmas during leave, he and Mom were married. A week after the wedding, Dad returned to the ship where he served another year. While on the *Franklin Roosevelt*, he was given a nickname — Holy Joe. Yes, my dad was one of those sailors who shared the gospel of Jesus Christ on his bunk, in the mess hall, on the deck, and on the street corners while in port. After serving his country he continued to preach at country churches every chance he got, while he worked full time for a trucking company as long as I can remember.

Fast-forward to December 1998: Dad retired in July when he turned 62. He and Mom had worked for years building their dream home at the lake. It was Christmas 1998 and we were all home for Christmas. After a wonderful dinner and exchanging gifts, we were standing in the kitchen when Dad's nose began to bleed. In that moment, life as we knew it changed forever. Dad said that he had not been feeling well, but he didn't want to worry Mom. He knew something was wrong. We could see it in his eyes. The very next week the doctor revealed it was cancer. Surgery was immediate and we prayed and hoped the cancer could be removed. However, the doctor came out and again . . . the news was not good. The cancer had spread to his liver and it was stage four colon cancer.

My dad, the man of faith that he was, said to us who were crying and distressed, "I am willing to endure anything if it is God's will, and if it will bring Him glory." We were in denial, but I think we all knew then the outcome did not look good. Dad was the strong one. He said, "If this is God's will, His purpose and plan for my life, then I will trust Him, no matter what the circumstance. Christ is enough."

The dream home they had built was unfortunately 250 miles from the hospital where Dad would be treated. Guess where the hospital was — in San Antonio, three miles from the home my husband and I shared. In that moment of disbelief with a plethora of questions, there was a reason to be thankful. Dad was right — God would provide. It's amazing how quick your needs change, both prayer and monetary. And there God is, in the hands and feet of His people who pray, serve, love, and care. Talk about Church Ladies! They came out of the woodwork — strangers we met in the hospital, our neighbors who had never met Dad, and the church . . . oh my goodness! Church Ladies brought meals and sent cards. Church men stopped by to pray while those back at their lake home took care of the yard and their house while they were at ours.

Everywhere we turned there seemed to be a ministry opportunity for Dad to share Christ. To nurses, doctors, hurting people in the waiting rooms (where it seemed we became a fixture), and always to those who came by to visit or pray. They left being encouraged by him. Never did I hear Dad complain, not even once! How can one be in so much pain, yet have such a grateful heart? Only God, we've discovered, can deliver peace, mercy, strength, and even joy in the midst of such calamity.

I'll never forget that day we brought Dad to our house. The drive from their home to ours was somber, like heels digging in with resistance then floating forward, and then again and again. It was hard, but you do what you have to, trusting God because in your pain and suffering, you don't really know what to do other than let go and let God.

Mom and Dad lived with us while Dad was taking chemo. They traveled back to their lake home as often as they could, which was a lot less than they had hoped for in the beginning. *Rollercoaster* became an overused word in our vocabulary. People praying and reaching out would take us up, and the bad test results would bring us down again. Through it all, God was victorious, and every bad day had a twinkle of hope, a heart that was thankful, and a supernatural joy that we knew could only come from the Lord Jesus.

"No eye has seen, no ear has heard, and no mind has imagined what God has prepared for those who love him" (1 Corinthians 2:9). My dad had always loved this passage of Scripture. During his illness, God opened my eyes and heart, that I would understand it. As I sat by Dad's bedside, questioning God one day, my heavenly Father seemed to shine His light on the rest of the passage, which I had never studied.

But people who aren't Christians can't understand these truths from God's Spirit. It all sounds foolish to them because only those who have the Spirit can understand what the Spirit means. We who have the Spirit understand these things, but others can't understand us at all. How could they? "Who can know the LORD's thoughts? Who knows enough to teach him? But we understand these things, for we have the mind of Christ" (1 Corinthians 2:16, NLT). On that day, the Lord opened my heart wide, and I got it! I had a renewed perspective on my dad's illness. While all we could think about was the loss, God had His best awaiting Dad. We should never expect to feel fully at home in this world because our real home is in heaven (Philippians 3:20). To be salt and light while here on this earth, we influence and illuminate the principles that Jesus taught. Although I had heard it all my life, this was an *aha* moment! God revealed to me that He would use Dad's suffering for His glory, and I could rest, find comfort and peace in that.

THE NIGHT MY DOG SAW ANGELS

It was our privilege to give the master bedroom to Mom and Dad. Bruce and I moved upstairs to the guest room while the master was downstairs. We set up a baby monitor, so if Mom or Dad needed us during the night, we could be there in a flash to help.

We had such precious times during these months. Spending time with Dad was a gift to our family. If you have known someone with cancer, you well know the ups and downs that come with this disease. A blessing, I'm sure, is the countless opportunity to love on and care for the one who is sick, being sure they have everything you can possibly give them to make their time comfortable and meaningful. Looking at it from Dad's perspective, he took every opportunity to share things about himself that we may not have known, or to make new memories to leave behind.

Although there are many stories that I love to share about these days with Dad, there are three that will forever be on my heart, those I believe the Lord wants me to share with you.

We found out that Dad had cancer in December 1998; it was now the first week of March 2000. The cancer had now taken my Dad's voice away. If you knew my Dad, you would understand that giving up driving, no longer signing his name, and beginning to have trouble speaking were reminders that this cancer was going to beat him. However, Dad told us in the very beginning, "I don't want to talk about the dying, only the living." We all agreed that, to our best ability, we would not talk about "the end" although we knew the end was near.

On this particular night, I was sleeping in the master with Mom; Dad was in the bed that hospice had brought over — in the same room, of course. About 2:00, I thought I heard something. I rose up to listen, and that's when I heard it again. Clear as a bell. "Honey!" Dad clearly spoke.

"Mom. Mom!" I nudged her. "It's Dad. Dad is calling for you."

We rolled out of bed and turned the light on. Now, you have to understand two things. One, it had been taking two, sometimes three of us to pull Dad up by that time. His muscles were weak and he had no strength; therefore, we had to lift him to sit or to stand. Two, my dad had only been able to whisper and was almost always too weak to carry on a conversation by this time. So to hear my dad speak seemed unreal for a moment, but the sound was sweet to our ears. Now, to see him sitting up on the side of the bed — wow! Now, that was a miracle and we all knew it!

Hospice had prepared us that the end was near. My sister, grandmother, two aunts, and cousin were all visiting. So when they heard Dad speak on the baby monitor, it sounded like a heard of buffaloes were coming down the stairs. In what felt like an instant, there we were, all standing around Dad's bed at 2:00 in the morning, greatly anticipating what would happen next!

I could feel my heart pounding inside my chest as we stood before him. And there he sat, looking intently at us with his white T-shirt tucked into his whitey tidies, legs crossed, rubbing his feet together, smiling from ear to ear. He appeared to be the strong, fun-loving, healthy dad I had known for 38 years.

"Dad, how are you sitting up?" I asked.

"They helped me." He smiled. "Look!" As he looked up and around, he raised his hands and stretched upward as if to touch something.

"What is it? What do you see?" Mom asked.

With a look of anguish, he replied, "Don't tell me you can't see them. Angels — they are all around us."

Again, he raised his hands up, stretched with all his might, turning around as though they surrounded the room.

"Daddy, what do they look like?" I asked with great anticipation.

"They are beautiful, iridescent. Colors that I can't describe. Every color and more than you have ever seen!"

I have to tell you that my dad didn't talk about angels. Nor had I ever heard him describe anything as iridescent. I'm sure of it!

Dad wanted so much to share this wonderful sight with us.

As we stood around him, I couldn't help but wonder, *Is this a dream?*

That's when it happened. Reeses, my nine-pound dachshund, who by the way had a special friendship with my dad, continued to jump up on my leg. My cousin Tammy saw her persistence and picked her up to hold her. The next thing we heard was Tammy saying, "Y'all look!"

Reeses was looking upward, tilting her head, as though she saw something there. We couldn't believe it! With her keen sense, could it be that she saw the angels too? No question, we were in the presence of angels; covered with Holy Ghost bumps (goose bumps), we were standing on holy ground.

My dad began to share with us what had happened: "Jesus helped me up, and He healed me. He told me that my new home is ready. I saw Mama and Daddy and others. They are there waiting for me." Then he said, "Doris is there too."

None of us could believe it! You see, Doris was their neighbor at the lake. She had passed away from a sudden heart attack the week before. Mom didn't tell Dad because she didn't want to upset him. This was no hallucination — it was real! Dad had a glimpse of heaven, and we felt as if we had too!

Then the sweetest thing happened. My dad patted the bed and looked at Mom. He motioned for her to sit down beside him. He looked into her eyes and said, "I love you." He put his hand on her cheek and he kissed her. He said as his voice slowly faded away, "I want you to go with me, but it's not your time."

Then he said, "I'm tired." As we helped him lay down, the life seemed to drain from his face and then from his body, as if he had been filled to full and then suddenly the plug had been pulled. As quick as it all started, it was over and Dad was asleep again.

It was an awesome night, one that each of us will remember forever. Everyone in the room that night was changed. If there had been any fear of dying, or any question that heaven is real, there was none now. My daddy, Joe Nelson, now calls Golden Street, Heaven, his home. And when God has finished preparing my heavenly home, I'll see him again. For now, I'm sure he is singing, "Holy, Holy, Holy" to the bright and morning star — King Jesus — which leads me to my next story.

That following week, Max and Denalyn, dear friends of ours, came over to sing to Dad. Max asked Dad if he had any requests. Dad wanted to say something, but he was having trouble. It seemed like he was listening intently, leaning upwards. He said, "Bright morning star. The choir is singing." Oh, he wants us to sing the hymn, "The Lily of the Valley, the bright and morning star," we thought. Dad shook his head no, but we sang it anyway. Dad was still trying to get something out and we just went on because he seemed to be frustrated. There was something he wanted to tell us but he couldn't find the words.

It wasn't until years later while studying the Book of Revelation, in the final words of the Bible, that I discovered these words: "I, Jesus, have sent my angel to give you this message for the churches. I am both the source of David and the heir to his throne. I am the bright morning star" (Revelation 22:16). In this passage of Scripture, Jesus says, "Yes, I am coming soon!" Then the writer says, "Amen! Come, Lord Jesus!"

Tears filled my eyes as I realized that Dad did have a request that day — to be in the presence of Jesus. Dad was ready to go home that day. Nothing else mattered. He was so close to heaven that he could hear the choirs singing, "Bright and morning star." What incredible hope that leaves you and me. That day, my eyes did see . . . once you have a glimpse of heaven, your earthly desires fade away and all that you long for is to be home with Jesus.

On March 24, I was leaving to speak at a girl's event. Dressed and packed, my things were ready to go. I was not. Torn, I sat on the bed beside my dad and I asked, "Daddy, should I go or should I stay here with you?" He shrugged his shoulders because he knew and I knew that his time on earth was short. I looked back at Mom and Bruce, hoping that someone would make the decision for me.

Then my dad said, "Come closer." Now, not only his voice a mere whisper, but his eyesight was just about gone. I got about two inches from his face, and amazingly he still had his quick wit. He said, "You're so pretty. You look just like me."

I smiled as the tears rolled down my face. "Daddy, I'll go, but I'm going to tell them about you and how you have been the best daddy ever."

He said, "No. Don't tell them about me. Tell them this ..."

We waited for the words as he thought. You could sense that what he wanted to say was very important. "Tell them (like most Baptist preachers, he had three points, so he held up three fingers), hurry up. Don't wait. Live for God."

My dad went home to Jesus while in our home in San Antonio on March 25, 2000. He was surrounded by loved ones as he took his final breath. At that same moment, I was standing in front of students in Encino, California, preaching his last message, encouraging them to come to Jesus, while Dad was meeting Him face-to-face. Although I got on the first flight out, it seemed like the jet engines were moving slower than ever that day. Leaning my head back against the seat, heaven seemed closer than ever. The bright blue sky with puffy white clouds were as pretty as a picture, and it was surreal knowing my dad, who had been lying in his bed just two days earlier, was there, in heaven, meeting Jesus face-to-face.

With an ache in my heart and a knot in my throat, feeling so alone on that plane was when it really hit me . . . my dad was gone! A part of me wanted to cry out loud, to shout it out to the other passengers, or to at least tell the lady sitting next to me that my dad had passed from this life into the next. Instead I sat silently. As I gazed through the heavens, God whispered, "*I love you and I am with you always.*" If anyone was watching me that day, they had to wonder, *What in the world is wrong with that girl? One minute she's crying and the next she's smiling.* Yes. I couldn't control it. A smile appeared on my face, and through the tears a sense of joy filled my heart. That was the moment when I thought back to a special day I had with Dad a few months earlier.

The good days seem to come and go. This particular day, Dad was feeling good. The girls were at school, Bruce at work, and Mom had gone to get her hair cut. I was in the kitchen cooking dinner when Dad called for me. "Sissy," he said. "Come sit by me for a while." We sat together in his big comfy chair-and-a-half, and he began to talk. As I listened, I remember thanking God for this sweet time, just me and my dad. First, he gave me his blessing for the new ministry I was preparing to establish. He thought it was very clever to call it GAB. He said, "Always be obedient to God's call. When God says go, you go. Don't worry about how. Just trust that He will provide when He calls. Always keep God first, then your marriage and family, then your ministry. People who aren't called will get tired easily. People who do ministry for selfish gain, they will fail and be miserable. But those who keep their focus on Him and keep their priorities in line, they will be blessed with passion and will never be happy doing anything else. It's not going to always make sense; but if God sets it into motion, if He opens the doors, then He will see it to completion. Take me, for instance. God has blessed me; He's been so good to me."

There was a pause and then his eyes got watery. "You know, I only have one regret in my life, and it's that I didn't trust God completely when He called me to pastor. Instead, I did it the way that seemed logical to me. I gave 110 percent at my job, but I was never really happy in my vocation; but when a door opened for me to preach . . . man, I enjoyed it! Preaching is what I was made to do. But instead of surrendering all, I gave most. I've done a lot of thinking lately, and we can't have it both ways. The truth is you're either obedient or you're not. Partial obedience or delayed obedience is still disobedience. I thought, *When I retire, then I can pastor a church.* And wouldn't you know, God has given me the desire of my heart. It's never too late to do His will. I retired, and He opened the door for me to pastor a church close to the house. Now my health fails me and that dream may never be fulfilled. I don't know . . . I can't make sense of it, but it's not for me to try. Only God knows the day and the hour, even the moment that He will call me home. For now I will press on like I'm going to live. I have surrendered all to His call and it's never too late for that. I'm at peace, and that's a good place to be."

We sat there for a little while, not saying a word, and I wondered, *Was it that he needed to confess his thoughts out loud? Or perhaps he was teaching me so I would recognize the importance of obedience in my own life? OR was it God's greater plan that I would be sharing his story with you?*

During his last months, Dad was ordained as a pastor. Church men and pastors that had mentored and loved him through the years laid hands on him and ordained him. Dad was frail, his skin was yellow, and he was weak, but the joy of the Lord was his strength. He could have canceled it. He could have stayed home in his bed — but instead he pressed on. The church was full of those who loved him. What an example of pressing on to the finish. Dad was humbled, blessed beyond measure, but His greater joy was that he knew God had made a way for him to fulfill his destiny.

Paul said,

> *"As for me, my life has already been poured out as an offering to God. The time of my death is near. I have fought the good fight, I have finished the race, and I have remained faithful. And now the prize awaits me"* (2 Timothy 4:6–8, NLT).

"Hurry up. Don't wait! Live for God." These were the last words I heard my dad say. What more could I ask for? My dad was a Christ follower, a church man. My heavenly Father used my dad's illness to teach me. The lesson — that God will fulfill His purpose in our lives, and it is not complete until the end. How wonderful to have the promise that this glorious conclusion of life here on earth is the beginning of eternal life with Him. "'For I know the plans I have for you,' declares the Lord, 'plans to prosper you and not to harm you, and give you hope and a future'" (Jeremiah 29:11).

The most important decision dad ever made was to accept the gift of God's grace through Jesus Christ. It is also the most important decision that you and I can make, because we have the promise of forgiveness and eternal life, and one day when we all get to Heaven, what a glorious day that will be!

During worship when we sing those old hymns, I can hear my daddy singing, "Tell me the story of Jesus; write on my heart every word. Tell me the story most precious, sweetest that ever was heard." It's my prayer that by sharing Dad's story, you recognize the most important story the Church Lady can ever share is His story, the story of Jesus, the story that gives power to the weak, sets the captives free, and promises eternal life to all who believe and call upon His name.

As I said in the beginning, I want to share with you something my dad shared with me. I pray you have heard it. I pray you will share it. It's the greatest story ever told and for every generation today, yesterday, and always!

"Therefore, go and make disciples of all nations, baptizing them in the name of the Father and of the Son and of the Holy Spirit, and teaching them to obey everything I have commanded you. And surely I am with you always, to the very end of the age" (Matthew 28:19–20). Most people are afraid to die. There is no need to fear death. You can have the assurance of Heaven today. Remember Dad's words: "Hurry up! Don't wait! Live for God!" Do it today!

- *"I have come that they may have life, and have it to the full"* (John 10:10).
- *"For the wages of sin is death, but the gift of God is eternal life in Christ Jesus our Lord"* (Romans 6:23).
- *"There is a way that appears to be right to a man, but in the end it leads to death"* (Proverbs 14:12).
- *"For Christ also suffered once for sins, the righteous for the unrighteous, to bring you to God"* (1 Peter 3:18).
- *"But God demonstrates his own love for us in this: while we were still sinners, Christ died for us"* (Romans 5:8).
- *"Here I am! I stand at the door and knock. If anyone hears my voice and opens the door, I will come in and eat with that person, and they with me"* (Revelation 3:20).
- *"If you confess with your mouth Jesus is Lord, and believe in your heart that God raised him from the dead, you will be saved"* (Romans 10:9).

The end for believers is just the beginning!

REVEAL AND TRANSFORM

1. Has there been a time recently that you shared in the happiness of another? And when were you blessed to have someone celebrate with you?

2. There is a lot of sadness in this world. Family members, neighbors, co-workers, etc. Who can you comfort that you have not?

3. Have you been faced with an illness and touched by the caring of Church Ladies? Explain.

4. Cancer seems to be more common than ever before, maybe because it has touched several in my own family. What is your response when someone has cancer?

5. Years ago there was a television show called *Touched by an Angel.* Have you ever noticed that Church Ladies seem to stand at attention with news of a terminal illness, a death, or a long-term illness? Have you been touched by a Church Lady? If so, how did her kindness bless you?

6. Let me encourage you to go when the Holy Spirit nudges you to send a card, make a phone call, send flowers, drive to treatments, clean a house, or provide a meal. Each one of these actions is God's love in action and appreciated more than you may ever know. Perhaps there is someone you can touch today. Any ideas?

7. Are you fearful of dying? If it's because you don't know where you will go when you take your last breath, believe that God's Word is true, and your faith in Christ will give you peace today. Write your thoughts, your fears, or concerns. If you, on the other hand, already have assurance of your eternal salvation, describe the peace you have about leaving this world and seeing Jesus face-to-face.

8. Has prayerfully hearing my dad's story helped you believe? Hurry up! Don't wait! Live for God today! Any thoughts, questions, or concerns?

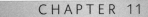

No Pedestals Allowed

Live in harmony with each other. Don't be too proud to enjoy the company of ordinary people. And don't think you know it all!

— ROMANS 12:16 (NLT)

It was a beautiful Sunday morning, but different than most. Instead of going to church we were on our way to a family celebration. On the drive over, I grumbled, "I just can't believe they are having the party at noon on Sunday. They should have had it on Saturday so we could go to church or at least later in the day." (As you can see, it was all about what worked best for me.) When we arrived, it was awkward. No one said hello! Or "We're so glad you're here." Instead we heard, "Wow! You mean you actually missed church today? I thought you guys might be too spiritual for us heathens." He laughed, and I knew he was joking, but his words really got to me. I didn't become defensive or let it ruin my day, but his rude welcome did cause the start of a spiritual self-evaluation within my heart.

Had we really given this impression? Had we become church snobs? Worse, had I become the infamous Church Lady as portrayed on a late-night TV show, so involved in church that we pushed others aside? True. Church activities did consume our lives; after all, isn't that what Christians are supposed to do? With church on Sunday morning and Sunday night, ladies Bible study on Tuesday, teaching aerobics on Mondays and Thursdays, Wednesday night supper and Bible study, not to mention all the children activities, we did have to say no to other opportunities. The more I thought about it, I realized we were never with the unchurched, unless we were knocking on their door at Tuesday night visitation. There was a check in my spirit, and I knew God was at work in my heart.

In *The Message*, Eugene Peterson puts Romans 12:14−16 in contemporary words: "Get along with each other; don't be stuck-up. Make friends with nobodies; don't be the great somebody." Oh my goodness! This was my worst nightmare — that someone could think I thought of myself as the great someone, holier-than-thou! "Lord Jesus, help me," I prayed.

I realized I had become so wrapped up in what was going on in the church building, that I was oblivious to the people outside the walls. Praise God that He allowed the joking words of a family member to cause an awakening in my spirit.

I turned to the Bible and began to search for direction and wisdom. As I studied and prayed, His purpose for my life became more defined, and it didn't include pedestals, that's for sure! My puffed-up heart had been deflated. With a heart of repentance, I trusted the Lord would take my mess and make it right.

Have you been there? To the place where people unimpressed with your good deeds sat you atop the pedestal of prideful Christians? It's ugly, I know. Unaware of the warnings, like a tsunami, pride can sweep us away before we know what hit us, especially if we're being swept away linking arms with those we're doing life with.

While living in my perfect little bubble (so I thought), unfortunately I dismissed those who weren't in the bubble with me. Honestly, as I began to seek the Lord on this, I didn't like what the Holy Spirit was revealing. Don't misunderstand — I've always loved Jesus and His people . . . or did I just love the people I hung out with, *church people?* I had really messed up. After all, His love in us should draw people to Him, not push them away. The problem was that I became so driven by *the doing* that my real purpose became fuzzy and watered down. I had good intentions, but my efforts to *get it all together* for God got in the way of what God was doing. Oh dear!

Christianity is having a personal relationship with Jesus Christ. Unfortunately, mine had become more about religion and denomination and less about relationship. Don't you know Satan loves this?

As I write, I have a visual. Me walking down a road, busy talking to my friends, trying so hard to do the right thing (God's Word plus man's opinion), so when the road came to Y with a huge blinking arrow that said *Christ followers this way*, I was distracted and I missed it! I never even noticed the Y or the sign, so I continue down the wrong path, farther away from God's will. Can you see the danger of too much religion? While it was my desire to be set apart for His glory, I was setting myself apart from Him!

Mercifully the Lord knew my heart. He loves me so much, that He knocked that pedestal of pride out from under me.

Why am I sharing this ugly story with you? Because when I read verse 16 of Romans 12, it was the first thing the Holy Spirit brought to my mind. I haven't thought about this in years. And I can't stop here, because what happened next shows what God did to get me back on the right road.

FOGGY GLASSES

Have you ever had glasses on when you took the lid off a pot of boiling water? The steam immediately fogs up your glasses. Well, let's just say I had been looking in that boiling pot way too long, and the Lord was lifting my head up, defogging my glasses (giving me a new perspective), and what I saw was troubling.

It was September, and Lindsey's sixth birthday was two weeks away. A few days after the invitations were mailed, I got several phone calls from concerned moms. They told me their child would not attend the party because they didn't want them exposed to New Age. What? I couldn't believe it! Much to my surprise they informed me the party theme Trolls had a mystical meaning. Should I change the theme? I was oblivious that the small cute toy had meaning at all. Lindsey simply liked the toy doll because they were cute and she could play with their crazy hair. I cried while Bruce thought it was absurd!

We discussed changing the theme, but in the end decided not to. We never said anything to Lindsey; and besides those few no-shows, the party was a fun time for all. We had a troll cake, troll napkins, and troll balloons. Lindsey wanted a troll with purple hair and a purple stone in its belly button and that was what she got. Believe me, it was a childhood fad; and if those little leprechauns had a hidden meaning, she never knew it.

That was the day I felt like we were being led out of the fog. We had gotten so well adjusted, so self-righteous that we hadn't noticed until now that we were following others down the path of legalism. Thankfully the Holy Spirit stopped us and got our attention while we still listened and were beginning to see what others had seen.

When it comes to children's birthday themes, we wondered, *Was there really a right or wrong here? Or was this the Lord allowing us to see legalism at work?* Legalism is binding—Christ sets us free! Legalism hurts people — Jesus loves people. I had to ask myself, *Would Jesus come to a child's birthday party if a plastic, purple-haired doll was sitting on top the cake?* I think He would.

In Galatians 5, Paul warns us that you cannot live in freedom and also under the legalism of the old law. Funny how still today believers say, "In Christ we are free"; however, in the next breath they judge another believer because they don't attend church on Sunday or don't dress right (in their eyes) for Sunday morning worship. It's important to note that legalism is also known as tradition or religion. While there is nothing wrong with keeping tradition, there is something wrong when someone holds that tradition over your head.

On this particular day in Galatians 5, the tradition being discussed was circumcision. Paul was speaking to the believers in Galatia, assuring the Jewish Christians (Jews who proclaimed Jesus as their Messiah) that being circumcised was of no value under the new regime. Nonetheless some of the leaders in the church were still teaching that the Gentiles must keep the old law in addition to believing in Jesus Christ. As you can imagine, it was causing confusion in the church. Paul taught that belief in Jesus Christ was enough. He quoted Jesus who said, "For the whole law can be summed up in this one command: 'Love your neighbor as yourself.' But if you are always biting and devouring one another, watch out! Beware of destroying one another" (vv. 14–15, NLT).

Paul was in essence trying to speak truth, hoping to keep the church in Galatia from splitting up. Unfortunately, some things never change. I've actually heard of a church that split because they couldn't agree on the color carpet to put in the new worship center. What must our heavenly Father think of His children? Disappointed, I am sure. But . . . His love is unending.

> "For if you are trying to make yourselves right with God by keeping the law [by working in the church], you have been cut off from Christ. You have fallen away from God's grace. But we who live by the Spirit eagerly wait to receive by faith the righteousness God has promised to us. For when we place our faith in Christ Jesus, there is no benefit in being circumcised or being

uncircumcised [a picture of legalism, doing something that is required by re-ligion]. What is important is faith expressing itself in love" (vv. 4–6, NLT).

The text goes on to say that God has called us to freedom. Paul uses the analogy of a little yeast being spread quickly through a whole batch of dough. Oh sister. When we become confused or troubled, we need to seek the truth and the truth will set us free. Believe me . . . I was seeking! In Luke 7:47, Jesus says that we who have been forgiven much must love much. The Father disciplines us because He loves us. The consequence for His forgiveness is an outpouring of His love.

It was now October, and our church was known for having a good Harvest Festival. This was a wonderful outreach and God was working in spite of His people. We invited our neighbors, and of course Lindsey and Holly always looked adorable in their costumes. But . . . on October 31, most of the members of our church turned off their porch lights and locked their doors.

We had prayed and were looking for opportunities to show His love with our neighbors. That's when we got this great idea. Bruce carved a funny face in one pumpkin and a cross on another while we talked to our girls about how God made pumpkins. Halloween night, we turned our porch light on. We handed out candy (the really good kind) and the girls and I made homemade pumpkin-shaped cookies for the adults. Our friends who had a problem with the troll really struggled with this! We, on the other hand, felt like we had escaped the pretentious bubble; and it felt good and right!

I made a poster for the door that said, *Ask about the Spirit who lives in this house.* And people did! We told them that the Spirit of God lives in our home because He lives in us. We played Sandi Patty kids music and it was a huge hit. We didn't pray with anyone, we didn't have anyone get saved on our porch, but love of Christ was shining through us to our neighbors.

This was it! God was teaching me how to love like He loves. We had been so busy with the first commandment that we hadn't followed through on the second — love your neighbor — that He says is equally important.

October 31 is now a night the Peeles look forward to. We don't go all-out now that the girls are grown up, but we do keep the light on, hand out candy, and prayerfully shine the love of Christ to all who approach our door. It's truly amazing how many people you get to know during the festivities of this night.

Don't be selfish; don't live to make a good impression on others. Be humble, thinking of others as better than yourself. Don't think only about your own affairs, but be interested in others, too, and what they are doing. (Philippians 2:3–4)

A LESSON LEARNED

Instead of being a light in the darkness, we had been keeping His light and love secure behind the walls of the church building. Isn't it wonderful that He, our heavenly Father, pursues us? I'm glad I heard Him and, believe me, He had my full attention. Thankful for His forgiveness and His mercy, He took my mess and made it beautiful. He was preparing this Church Lady for a new day!

Aren't you thankful the Lord came to rescue us from ourselves? He comes to our rescue, showers us with His grace, and loves us more than we can imagine. Agape love is divine love.

Dear friends, let us love one another, for love comes from God. Everyone who loves has been born of God and knows God. Whoever does not love does not know God, because God is love. (1 John 4:7–8)

My story is raw and real. Ugly as it may be, I trust the Lord will use it for His glory. If nothing else, it reminds me how easy it is for me to be ungodly and, even more so, how much I need a Savior.

Have you gotten caught up in self-righteous living? The word explains itself: *self-right.* Then you know how it feels to be forgiven and freed when His righteousness is what we seek. Praise God for new beginnings!

Jesus said, "For whoever wants to save their life will lose it, but whoever loses his life for Me will save it" (Luke 9:24). Jesus said, "Come follow me." The Christian life is truly a great adventure when we follow Him!

Months later, Bruce's employer transferred us to San Antonio. We embraced the opportunity. God had prepared us for change. We didn't know anyone in San Antonio. The first thing we did was get to know our neighbors. We didn't just wave at them as we rushed in our home. We had block parties, played games in our front yards, took time to be interested in what they were doing, celebrated babies, went to first communions and baptisms (in churches other than our own), and in the midst of doing life together, we were blessed and God was glorified. It was during this move where God showed me I'm just an ordinary girl, with an ordinary family, living an ordinary life . . . just like my neighbors. Aren't you glad to know that God uses ordinary people to do extraordinary things? The Bible is full of stories about ordinary people.

LUNCH AT THE BAR

Years later, now living in Houston, it was a typical Saturday afternoon, and Bruce asked the famous question, "Where do you want to eat lunch?" Usually my response is, "I don't care." That answer drives Bruce crazy! But on this day I knew exactly where I wanted to have lunch — Pappasito's, the best Mexican food restaurant in town. It was crowded, and we were hungry. The hostess said, "There's a 45-minute wait or there are two stools available at the bar." We looked at each other and agreed — *Let's do it!* Believe me, this was a big deal. Five years earlier, we would have waited the 45 minutes and looked at the hostess like *are you serious?*

The bartender asked what we wanted to drink. Bruce said, "Two teas, please."

"Two teas, coming up. How are y'all today?" the young man asked.

"We're great! How is your day going?" As we enjoyed our chips and queso, he told us that he was a college student working his way through school.

Bruce said, "Good for you!"

"Yeah, but my social life sucks," he said.

"Aww. That's no good. Our two girls just came here after graduating from college, so your story is a familiar one. Do you go to church, by chance?" I asked casually while stuffing another chip in my mouth.

"Well, funny you should bring that up. I've been feeling like I should get connected with a church, but I really just haven't taken the time. I went to church as a kid but it's been a while. I'm 25 and tired of the party scene."

He sat our delicious-smelling fajitas in front of us, and as he walked away, Bruce prayed as we always do.

When he came back over he asked us a few questions about our daughters — where they went to school, and so on — which was the perfect opportunity for us to say more.

"Since we had moved to Houston while they were in college, they didn't know anyone here. They started going to a church not far from here and they've made some great friends; lifelong friends, I'm sure," I said.

He wanted to know the name of the church. When I told him, he said, "Yeah, that's the church I always drive by and feel something inside saying . . . *you need to check it out.*"

"See, God works in mysterious ways, anything to get our attention," I said. "We have never eaten lunch at a bar, but I bet the Lord sat us down right here to encourage you today."

"Yes ma'am," he said as he stuck out his hand. "Maybe you'll see me there."

"Well, wasn't that special? We sat at the bar and got to talk about the Lord," I said to Bruce as I skipped to the car. (Not really, but I was pretty excited!)

When we take time to listen to others, it doesn't take a psychologist to figure out that we're all ordinary. It's when we live life in the fast lane, misguided by the culture and man-made religion, that we lose the simple act of loving people.

Aren't you relieved to know there is no such thing as the *perfect* Church Lady? Seriously, no matter how hard you try, *it just ain't gonna happen*! It's called freedom, sister — the kind Paul talks about in Galatians 5:1: "It is for freedom that Christ has set us free. Stand firm, then, and do not let yourselves be burdened again by a yoke of slavery." Man-made traditions can keep us stuck in the rut of opinion; it's unfortunate that some of these age-old traditions have kept us from knowing and doing the will of God.

When we believe that God loves the whole world (that included everyone), only then can we begin to recognize how small we are and how big He is! God specializes in losers and mess-ups — imperfect people. He loves us unconditionally! (See John 3:16.) Jesus is our perfect example, yet He knows we will never attain perfection. Knowing this, He still created us to be a part of His big plan. It's amazing, isn't it?

Think about the people Jesus hung out with when He lived among us. He played with the children, enjoyed conversation with Mary and Martha, blessed the poor widow, listened to the prostitute, touched the leper, and ate with the one who betrayed Him. Just flip through the pages of the New Testament and you'll see: God uses ordinary people like you and like me.

SHATTERING THE STEREOTYPE

Years ago the Church Lady had a starring role on a popular late-night television show. Unfortunately, she was portrayed as self-righteous, judgmental, unloving, and legalistic by the producer who so cleverly stereotyped her character. It was hilarious, and we laughed. No Christian woman sets out to demonstrate this negative Church Lady character so . . . we are breaking that mold, shattering the stereotype! This fictional character may have exposed some ungodly characteristics, but praise God, the Holy Spirit made us mindful of that condescending spirit, and the Father of us Church Ladies says we're taking it back! We are the real Church Ladies and we are going to love the world in spite of ourselves.

I don't know about you, but I'm thankful the Father continues to refine me, to humble me, and to make me more like Him. Lesson learned! Don't be selfish; don't live to make a good impression on others. Be humble, thinking of others as better than yourself (Philippians 2:3).

When we are up on the mountaintop, it's wonderful, yes, but there's not much room up there, and most of the time it's an experience that is enjoyed by few. It's when we are climbing up the mountain that we notice those around us, doing life beside us. If we love them because He first loved us, then they will see the real traits of a Church Lady. Perhaps they will say, "Look, there's that Church Lady. She loves Jesus, she can help, or she'll accept me, or she'll encourage me, she'll love me, she'll pray with me, she'll _____ ." And Church Ladies will reach out even when it's not convenient — not what we had planned for our day, not our spiritual gift, not our way or tradition.

> Because God chose you to be the holy people He loves, you must clothe yourselves with tenderhearted mercy, kindness, humility, gentleness, and patience. Make allowances for each other's faults, forgive each other — most importantly, love is what binds us together in perfect harmony. The peace of Christ will rule our hearts. For as members of one body, you are all called to live in peace. And always be thankful. (Colossians 3:12–15)

What do you think? Can you see why the Lord wants you to embrace who you are, His daughter, the Church Lady? Can you see Him purifying you, refining, pruning, molding, whatever it takes for you to shine His gospel message to the world? There is a song that says, "People, get ready.

Jesus is coming. Soon we'll be going home." If the time is at hand — and it is — together we can shine brighter, not by gritting our teeth, but with glory strength, the strength He gives. "It is strength that endures the unendurable and spills over into joy, thanking the Father who makes us strong enough to take part in everything bright and beautiful that he has for us" (Colossians 1:11–12 *The Message*).

Share His love at work, to our neighbors, to our children, to our husbands, to our schools, at the grocery store, to strangers, to ordinary people, to everyone, to the world!

If this is a wake-up call, are you awake? God is calling His church — more specifically His Church Ladies — to rise up. When we are recognized because of our love, what we do and say, how we reflect Christ — not by who we are, but whose we are — He is glorified! What a privilege to be called *the Church Lady*.

My name is Chandra Peele and I am a Church Lady. Ordinary as one can be, believing God will do extraordinary works in me!

REVEAL AND TRANSFORM

1. Is the Holy Spirit revealing legalism or judgmental thoughts today?

2. In your ordinary self, how is the Lord using you for extraordinary purposes?

3. Were you convicted, changed, or moved by my honesty? How?

4. Have you had a similar circumstance, a time when the Holy Spirit revealed that your religious opinions caused others to step away from His church instead of being drawn into it?

5. Write your thoughts after each statement:

   Live in harmony with each other.

   Don't try to act important.

   Enjoy the company of ordinary people.

   And don't think you know it all.

6. Isn't it great to know we are a work in progress? Praise God He's still working on us, molding and shaping us to look and love more and more like Him. Regarding this chapter, where specifically is the Lord at work in your heart today?

7. Have you ever put yourself above others? Did you realize it, or was it brought to your attention? What did you change to get yourself back on track?

8. Pride — it's a hard thing to admit when yours gets hurt. Do you easily admit when you are wrong? Pray the Holy Spirit gently reveals your prideful ways before you experience that long fall from prideful, back to ordinary.

9. What is the greatest message you will take from this chapter?

10. Is God calling you to change something, and if so, what?

CHAPTER 12

Hurt by the Church Lady

Never pay back evil with more evil.
Do things in such a way that everyone can see you are honorable.

— ROMANS 12:17 (NLT)

eliverance! What a feeling worthy of praise! To be set free from something that has bound you for weeks, months, possibly years . . . now that's worthy of a *hallelujah* shout!

Surely you too have experienced the darkness of perplexity? From my experience, nothing has tested my character and judgment greater than having another believer wrongly blame me or to speak of me untruthfully. But it happens. And it happened to me.

I think you will agree that when there is dissension between people, the tiniest spark can quickly get out of hand, like a wildfire that destroys everything in its path. The truth is, when we are not motivated by love, we are quick to be critical of others. Unfortunately, we've all been on both sides of this coin.

After being a churchgoing girl my whole life, I know that Church Ladies can get their feelings hurt over the littlest things. Unfortunately, I've been there, done that. With age comes wisdom, and over the years I've learned to be more selective in what I share. However, sometimes my mouth is already open to speak when I feel that check in my spirit say, "Keep your mouth shut!" And the dreaded words come rolling off my tongue.

Believe me, there have been plenty of times that I begged God for a do-over. He continues to teach me "godly mouth etiquette." For a girl who loves to talk, trust me, I'm still learning. Currently He is teaching me to pause before I react. I tend to jump the gun, to reply or respond too quick, but I'm working on it.

Unfortunately, there have been times when I completely missed His nudging and have turned a deaf ear to that check in my spirit. Knowing there has been spiritual growth in the providence of loss inspires me even more to put my trust in Him alone. I've learned along the journey not to assume that I have the knowledge to execute any plan, instead I trust that He will go before me and lead the way. I can surely testify that "all things work together" if He is in control. And when things don't seem to be working out, I've learned to step back, be still, and wait for Him before I make my next move.

I've actually had this modeled by a couple who are truly in love with Jesus Christ. They love Him with their whole heart, and it is evident in every area of their life. Max and Denalyn Lucado are wonderful role models of God's kindness toward others. They seem to move with God, diligently aware of who they are and who they are not. They both have a gentle spirit and a way of saying little, but making such an impact in the world around them. Years ago, I witnessed their response when others spoke disheartening words about their ministry. They pressed on, keeping their eye on the goal — God's purpose. When it was over, and the dust settled, they were standing strong, and God continues to pour out His favor on them, their family, and their ministry.

I don't know about you, but when someone hurts me or hurts someone I love, my first thought is to defend myself or my loved one. It's hard not to harbor the hurt. The Lucados gave it to God from the moment hurtful words were encountered. While I have been blessed by their "living it out," Jesus is our greatest example when we consider all the times He could have defended Himself, but instead He said nothing or He prayed, "Father, forgive them, for they know not what they do" (Luke 23:34, NLT).

MY STORY

Growing up, the people at my church were my extended family. We loved each other, prayed for each other, sang, "I'm so glad I'm a part of the family of God," every Sunday evening and I believed it! We were with our church family a minimum of three times a week. We played together, prayed together, and laughed and cried together. These people knew me well, they loved me, and I loved them! You never imagine that one of these people could — or would, for that matter — hurt you.

Then one day, my seemingly "perfect church world" was rocked, knocked off its axle. That was the day my *church world* bubble landed on a tack and burst. It was the day I realized *Church Ladies aren't perfect!* As much as I went to church, I should have known better. Jesus Christ is the only perfect One. But still, I thought as I cried, "*God, how could a sister in Christ, a Church Lady, hurt me like this?*"

Of course, my greatest focus quickly became all about me, and I failed to recognize that Jesus Himself had been betrayed and falsely accused many times in His 33 years. And most often it was by those who were closest to Him, who surely loved Him. When you read about Peter's denial (Matthew 26:69–75), you too must wonder how he could have been so cruel. But he was. Jesus knew that Peter would deny Him three times before the rooster crowed, the same way He knows that you and I in our humanness, in our sinful nature, will naturally put self first and others last. For this reason, He tells us over and over that we must deny ourselves and put others first. Our Father knows that if we can willingly do this one thing, we can experience greater freedom and our lives will reflect His Son more. But we fail. We fail over and over, again and again, yet He forgives us.

Have you ever been hurt by someone in church?

Now the really tough question: have you ever hurt someone in church?

You can't really talk about the issue without admitting that you, too, have fallen short of the "love your neighbor" command. It's easy to think a little gossip now and then is not that significant. And surely just listening to gossip would go unnoticed — no. It is what it is — sin. Gossip, jealousy, and even adding to the truth will eventually hurt someone. Jesus said, "If you hold to my teaching, you are really my disciples. Then you will know the truth, and the truth will set you free" (John 8:31–32). Jesus is the Truth. Only Jesus can set us free from the consequences of sin. That is why little white lies (there's no such thing) and gossip are so ugly and the fallout so terribly hurtful. Remember, half the truth is a whole lie.

When we belong to Christ, God is continually working in us to purify our heart. Therefore, He isn't going to sit back and let us spin out of control. He will discipline us like a loving Father does his children (no matter how old we are) to get us moving in the right direction — over and over, if that's what it takes to shape us into the person He created us to be, for the purpose He has appointed to us. Only then will we be set free from the agony and pain that go hand and hand with sin. Jesus tells us in John 14:15–17,

> *"If you love me, keep my commands. And I will ask the Father, and he will give you another advocate to help you and be with you forever — the Spirit of truth. The world cannot accept him, because it neither sees him nor knows him. But you know him, for he lives with you and will be in you."*

You may be thinking, "Oh no. I didn't sign up for all this!" Yes, you did! And remember, nothing is hidden from the Father. He knows every thought that you have. Believe me, I've gone through His discipline many times in my life, and from what I read in the Bible, we His children will continue to be refined until He calls us home. Truly, His refining and pruning is a good thing.

It gets a little uncomfortable when we talk about sin, doesn't it? We can talk about murder, adultery, and bank robbers; but when we talk about telling lies, adding to the truth, and gossip, it hits closer to home, and we feel that squirming, unsettled feeling inside. It's because God is at work. In the same way, we Church Ladies don't really like to talk about the ugliness that goes on in the church with church people. Why? Because we want to keep that "perfect image" in our mind like I had as a child.

Here's the church, here's the steeple, open the doors, and see all the *perfect* people!

In reality *we the church* are truly a bunch of ordinary people, with human flaws like the rest of the world. Praise God that Christ followers — that would be me and prayerfully you — are being made new in Him, and *that* is what makes us different than those who are not Christ followers. Jesus also clearly teaches that the one who is forgiven much should forgive much.

HURTFUL WORDS

At the time, I was a student minister, and summers were packed with missions trips, camps, fellowship, lock-ins, and door-to-door evangelism. It was a hot summer afternoon when the bus pulled in from youth camp. We had truly experienced God during all the fun, but more importantly through corporate worship, Bible study, and a week of being in the company of other believers. We were all ready to get home, exhausted from the camp experience, and quite frankly I was ready to sleep in my own bed and enjoy the luxury of my own personal bathroom.

Summer camp is often described as a mountaintop experience — a time to get out of your comfort zone and surround yourself with Jesus freaks who have the freedom to "get real" with Jesus. At this particular camp, we witnessed many who publicly accepted Jesus Christ as their Lord and Savior. For others it was a time of spiritual renewal.

One night after the worship service, one of our staff kids came to me and shared how she really believed that her childhood profession of faith was just an action, something she did at Vacation Bible School because everyone else was doing it. With tears in her eyes, she shared that she had prayed for assurance of her salvation that night and that she wanted to be re-baptized at church once we got back home. Fearful of sharing the news with her mom, she asked if I would pray with her. She had a feeling that her mom would not understand or support her decision and that she might even be embarrassed. She shared that she didn't want to disappoint her mom; however, she felt that this was what God was leading her to do. Either way, she knew God knew her heart. Excited for her, I prayed and asked the Lord to soften her mom's heart so that she would be ready to hear and respond gratefully to this decision.

The following week, this young lady came to my office and wanted me to go with her to share the news with her mom because she was hoping to be baptized the next Sunday. Unfortunately, the daughter's intuition was correct: while sharing the news with her mom, her body language clearly showed disappointment. With her arms crossed, she looked at her daughter, and then at me, and strongly expressed how once you are saved you are always saved and that the daughter had made her decision to follow Christ at five years old. The daughter looked at me for help. I simply shared with her mother the words that her daughter had shared with me at camp. Suddenly, the mom became angry and said that I had done something to cause her daughter to doubt her salvation and that she would *not* be getting re-baptized.

When I left her office, the daughter looked at me through tearful eyes as though to say, "I told you this is how she would react."

I went home, shared what had happened with Bruce, and we prayed for the mom and the daughter. I loved this family and was taken aback by the situation. The next day, our pastor called me into his office. Walking from my office to his, I couldn't help but wonder what the unexpected meeting was about. Funny, but being called to the pastor's office was always a bit intimidating. As I made my way to his office, I couldn't help but wonder if it was something to do with what had happened at camp.

The pastor began to tell me that this mother was very upset with me. In fact, she was so upset, that she said if he didn't fire me, she would leave the church. Suddenly it seemed the wind was knocked out of me, or perhaps more like a dagger had been plunged deep into my heart. Then a knot the size of a golf ball seemed to swell up in my throat and I couldn't speak. I was shocked! In disbelief! I couldn't imagine her being so upset. Instantly I began to search my heart and beg God to shine His light on anything I may have done that was worthy of this meeting.

God continued to take me back to the truth and it was actually very simple: this student had come to me to express her sincere desire to be baptized because she wanted to make a public statement of her faith, one that she meant and understood.

Could it really be that this mom was this upset by her daughter's decision to be re-baptized? Well, I guess I'll never know. The pastor did not fire me, and like she had said, she resigned and left the church the next day. Just like that!

Hearing that she had resigned, I felt sick to my stomach. I wanted to speak with her but she refused my attempts. Being the woman I am by nature, I wanted to get to the bottom of it. I wanted to talk about it. She, on the other hand, had the opposite personality, and I'm guessing she was stewing in her heart and did not want to speak to me. So what did I do next? I went to talk with her co-workers at church. I was so distraught over this that I couldn't sleep. I needed to get this settled. People began to talk in the church, and I felt a burning need to clear myself. I tried to go about my job, but I had allowed this mess to consume my every thought. The next thing I knew I was being falsely accused of something else, which was rumored to be the real reason this mom wanted me terminated immediately. Yes — there was *drama in the church*.

Go back and count the *I*'s in the last paragraph. Whew! There are a lot of them. That is exactly what happens when gossip and lies begin. When we try to defend ourselves, our world becomes all about us instead of all about

Him. Do you realize there is no such thing as she *hurt my feelings*? No. What actually happened was she *hurt my pride*; therefore, my emotions were going crazy and I felt the need to react. We can react silently, or we can react loudly.

For weeks, each time I would say anything to defend myself, the story seemed to grow and create more trouble. Desperate to hear from God, I began to spend a lot of time on my knees. One day, in that position of prayer, the Holy Spirit led me to this verse:

> *Do everything without grumbling or arguing, so that you may become blameless and pure, children of God without fault in a warped and crooked generation. Then you will shine among them like stars in the sky as you hold firmly to the word of life.* (Philippians 2:14–16)

In my time of desperation, God reminded me that Jesus Christ, His Son, had not only been falsely accused but had been spit upon, cursed, beaten, whipped, and hung on a cross. And what was his attitude? "Father, forgive them." The death of our Savior Jesus Christ is surely the greatest example of forgiveness, and before His death, Jesus taught about forgiveness many times. In Matthew 18:21–22, Peter asked Jesus, "'Lord, how many times shall I forgive my brother or sister who sins against me? Up to seven times?' Jesus said, 'I tell you, not seven times but seventy-seven times'." Then He compared the kingdom of heaven to a master who wanted his servant to settle his very large debt. The servant begged him to give him more time. The Master took pity on the man and canceled his debt.

Can you imagine if someone came to you today and forgave all your debt? And this was a large debt in that day! After such a gift you would certainly become giving and forgiving, right? Not everyone would show their gratitude in the same way. Jesus goes on to say the very same servant who had just received this merciful gift of financial freedom went straight to one of his servants who owed him a debt and demanded immediate payment. When he heard that his servant could not repay him, he grabbed him, choked him, and sent him to prison. Astounded by what they saw, the other servants reported this back to the master who had forgiven this man's debt. Disappointed in his actions, the master confronted the servant and sent him to prison. To finish the story, Jesus said, "This is how my heavenly Father will treat each of you unless you forgive your brother and sister *from your heart*" (v. 35).

Jesus tells us how believers should respond when there is a conflict (Matthew 18:15–20). We should go to that person and try to come to an agreement. If the sister will not listen or doesn't want to talk about it, only then should we bring one or two witnesses along. If she still refuses to listen, we should take it before the church. And if she refuses to listen to the church, we should know that we tried to take care of it God's way and let it go, let her go. When we try to take care of problems God's way, it will have a positive impact. It may not happen the way we would want it to, but in the end it will have a positive impact. If we Church Ladies would only consider God's Word and direction in this area, there would be less heartache in our lives. When we have a heart of repentance, only then can we bathe in the mercy of God.

It wasn't long after being hurt by this Church Lady that God released me and my family from that particular church fellowship. Although my heart was broken in a million pieces (many of those pieces seemed to get left on the floors of that church building), I knew God was leading us to go. "Why is this happening, God?" I cried out many times. We had wonderful memories, had made precious friendships through the years, I had served there on staff, my children grew up there, and I had grown up spiritually with this body of believers. There was so much "Peele history" there. Deep within me there was an unexplainable peace, a soft spoken word — *go*. So we did.

Little did I know that God was taking us away because more heartache was about to enter that church family. Having recently resigned, my name once again was implemented. Satan was at work . . . big time! Only by the grace of God were people hearing the gospel, being fed and growing in their faith. God is greater than everything! How awesome to know that when we falter, He is solid, the foundation that cannot be shaken.

Desperately wanting to clear my name, the Lord made it clear for Bruce and me to be silent. "Vengeance is mine," says the Lord. *Don't hit back; discover beauty in everyone.* Whoa — that's impossible in our own strength. *If you've got it in you, get along with everybody.* Well, I try to. *Don't insist on getting even; that's not for you to do. I'll do the judging. I'll take care of it.* For these words we were so thankful.

We believed God for that promise and backed away from relationships we had made through the years, which were now strained. So hurtful, so sad! This was the darkest time of my life — a valley so deep, a time of perplexity and confusion, not of my heart but of my mind. No doubt

Satan was having a heyday! It was huge, ugly — lies, gossip, rumors, sin! In the church!

If I had ever experienced suffering, it was then, the pain some days so great I didn't want to leave my bed. Like a dark cloud over my body, I felt as though I had run into a spiritual fog bank and that I was all alone.

One day, again on my knees, I heard the Lord, say, *Don't fight it. Be still and know that I am God. The storm may feel bitter, cold, dark, and unending, but I'm with you, holding you tight in the grip of my hand. Hold out! There will be an end and you will come out stronger on the other side.* So frail and timid, I placed my hand in His and prayed that He would hold me and keep me safe from this ugly raging storm that seemed to be drowning me.

One of the first things my family needed to do was to find a new church in the area. The "place to be" for students was a community Bible church in town. But . . . that was the church where *the lady*, the one who had resigned because of me, was now attending. So of course we couldn't go there! Did I pray about that decision? No! We joined another church in the area, and although the preacher was anointed and a dear friend and the people were kind, we never seemed to fit in. We never could think of a good reason, other than God had us there to heal for a season. After four years of trying, it was obvious that this was not the church where God wanted us to serve. One Sunday morning while getting dressed for church, our daughter Holly said, "Can we please visit CBC?" Bruce agreed that we should visit. He said that the church was so huge we would probably never see "this particular Church Lady."

We walked into church, the four of us side by side, and it felt like a scene out of a movie. The 200-plus choir was singing, the Spirit of God was present, and in that moment we all looked at each other with tears in our eyes. It seemed as though God said, "Welcome home!" After the congregation sang a couple of praise songs, the worship leader instructed us to welcome those around us. In that moment time stood still. As I shook the person's hand in front of me, there she was, two rows directly in front of me. I wanted to practice stop, drop, and roll . . . right out the door. But instead I grabbed Bruce by the arm and pointed to her. He smiled with a nervous disbelief. "Six thousand people in the church and we *just happen* to sit two rows directly behind her?" he whispered. "I don't think so. This was a divine situation."

After avoiding this woman for all these years, God had a plan. And to think, if I had gone to *that* church in the first place, it would have saved me from years of heartache. God knew this was where I needed to be, and like Jonah, I ran the other way. The following Sunday, we visited again. This time we went to another area to sit, assuming that surely we could avoid a run-in. Nope! Instead, her husband was the usher in that area and he greeted us with a smile. "Hello, how are the Peeles?" he said as he walked us down the aisle to our seats. Again we were amazed! After the service began, I watched him carefully to see where he would sit, knowing that she would be sitting there too. Sure enough, they sat five rows in front of us on the opposite side of the aisle. During the meet-and-greet time, she turned around and we made eye contact, so we waved to each other. Awkward! The message that morning spoke directly to me. It was titled "Leaving the Past in the Past." Later that week I got her phone number from a mutual friend and I prayed earnestly before I called her. After the third ring on a recording, she said the all-familiar "leave a message after the beep." I wanted to hang up, but I didn't. Instead, I left a message with my number and asked her to call me back. You know . . . she never did. And I was OK with that. After that we rarely saw each other at church; and if we did, we smiled. I'd always hoped that was her way of saying, "It's OK; let's just leave it in the past."

A few months went by, and on a Saturday evening after church service, we noticed our pastor walking out another door. We waved and, much to our surprise, he turned and walked toward us; really nice guy, so down to earth. We talked for only a few moments, but what happened in those few moments was life-changing. I asked him to pray for us because we had been hurt in our last church and we couldn't seem to shake it. He looked at me and said, "Chandra, how long has that been?"

I said, "Almost five years."

He simply replied, "Wow! The Israelites only have 35 years on you. Let it go!" His words were few but powerful!

This meeting wasn't a coincidence, it was divine! I realized in that moment that I had allowed this hurt to consume me, to steal my joy, to keep me focused on me and from serving where God wanted me to *for five years*. At this point I was choosing to hurt myself and there was nothing God-honoring about it! Instead I was allowing Satan to keep a hold on me, my thoughts, and my life.

Like a bird being released from its cage, I was set free! Five years of suffering was finally over. While thanking God for the words my pastor had spoken, I pondered the past five years, like flipping through a photo album, a collection of pictures and events in my mind. I was reminded of the hurt, the loneliness, self-pity, depression, clouded judgment, all which leads to false conclusions. Satan knocked me down, I felt defeated, and I let him win the battle for five years! Like clearing the hard drive on my computer, I pushed "erase," gave it up to the Lord for good, and in that moment it was gone as quickly as it had come into my life. *Cleansing and freedom are birthed out of forgiveness. And I received it!* In the end, God won the battle! "My grace is all you need. My power works best in weakness." (2 Corinthians 12:9, NLT).

During those dark days, I met with God more than at any other time in my life. I read and studied the life of Paul which brought me comfort. I had become totally dependent on the Lord, desperate for His help in my time of need. The more I suffered, the more comfort the Lord gave me. I lost some friends, but I gained so much more — a closer relationship with Jesus, my Savior, my first love and best friend. I have forgiven all those who hurt me and who falsely accused me. Shortly after breaking free from what seemed to be irreconcilable differences, God began to reconcile. I was able to speak with those I had offended and asked them to forgive me. The few who wouldn't talk to me, I had to leave in God's hands and move forward. He had healed me and I'm not wasting anymore time stuck in this muck and yuck. I'm free! Free indeed!

This season of my life wasn't pretty; in fact, it was ugly! Looking back, God taught me so much during this difficult time. He taught me the power of humility, what it means to turn the other cheek, the freedom that comes with trusting Him alone, the joy that comes from obedience, and the indescribable peace that follows truth. Each of these lessons learned brought me closer to Him. Once I put my focus back on Christ, the freedom I began to experience gave me a greater desire to serve Him through reaching out to others. I'm a better listener and more attentive to hurting people. I've got my joy back and it feels so good!

In Philippians 4:4–5, Paul encourages believers to "always be full of joy in the Lord. I say it again — rejoice! Let everyone see that you are considerate in all you do. Remember, the Lord is coming soon" (NLT). If only I had allowed the joy of the Lord to outweigh the hurt, but I didn't. Instead, I let my hurt feelings dictate my actions and steal my joy.

The Father knows best, and when He needs to get our attention, could it be that He permits us to stumble so we can fall at His feet? There, we are vulnerable, desperate, and dependent on Him alone. At His feet is often where we attain depth and spiritual growth. Our loving and merciful Father is faithful to do whatever it takes to help us find our way through the hairpin turns of darkness back into the path of righteousness. When we allow our problems, worries, and heartache to consume us, our vision becomes blurred. Like a pot of simmering spaghetti when left unattended, it splatters everywhere and gets messy, creating hurt for everyone involved. So, from my experience, don't hold onto past hurts — lay it at His feet today!

Looking back on those five years, I can say it was all worth it! There is no question that my relationship with the Lord became stronger during that dry season. God was there to hold me, to listen, and to teach me during the silence. Even when I didn't know what to pray, He did his work through my nothingness.

What about you? Do you need to forgive someone today? Don't let Satan steal your joy for another second. Trust God to make what is wrong right. No matter your situation, God wants you to know that you should rest in Him. He is in control of your situation, just like He was in mine. Perhaps He will say, "Lay it at My feet, forget about it, and move on." Or maybe He will nudge you to talk with that person. Or perhaps He will lead you to trust Him and say nothing at all.

If you are going through the refining fire, it's difficult, it hurts, perhaps you don't understand why this is happening to you. Hold on, Church Lady, God has a plan. He is good, He's still on His throne, and He's still in love with you. When you get on the other side of hurt, you'll recognize more than ever before the joy of the Lord and the sweetness of freedom.

Reveal and Transform

What I learned:
- Christian people make mistakes.
- Always speak the truth.
- Don't share everything you know, especially if it's about someone else.
- When facing conflict, don't let pride get in the way.

- Be obedient even when what the Lord asked you to do doesn't seem easy.
- When you can't find your way, trust Him and His timing.
- When you're lonely and powerless, study the Word and talk to God.
- Forgive much and admit your wrongs.
- God will give you the strength to endure when you depend on Him alone.
- When everything and everyone is gone, you still have all that you need in Christ!

1. Read 2 Corinthians 12:7–10. God refused to remove Paul's thorn. We don't know exactly what Paul's thorn in the flesh was, but we do know it was a hindrance to his ministry. The thorn kept Paul humble, reminded him of his need for constant contact with God, and it benefited those around him as they saw God at work in Paul's life.

   What is/was your thorn, and how might/did God use it to keep you humble?

2. Read Philippians 4:6–9. What is the Lord saying to you through His Word?

3. Read 1 Peter 5:6–11. Be encouraged!

The Real Thing!

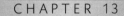

*Instead, if your enemies are hungry, feed them. If they are thirsty,
give them something to drink. [Conquer] evil by doing good.*

— ROMANS 12:20–21 (NLT)

The Peele family was on vacation. And on this particular day, other than getting Bruce a hot dog from a famous street vendor and finding designer handbags for us girls, the day was ours to explore the Big Apple.

Excited about our excursion, the concierge gave us a few last-minute tips. She informed us there is a difference between a fake and a knockoff. A fake is obvious. A knockoff, however, is so close to the real thing that most people cannot tell the difference. Well, of course we wanted the knockoff. She drew us a map to a place where she knew had the best deals. We girls could hardly wait to find our treasure. Bruce, on the other hand, would have preferred to stay at the hotel, but came along as our bodyguard. Of course we never dreamed we would actually need one.

We walked down eight blocks and turned right like she had instructed. However, after one turn we quickly found ourselves on an empty street on the outskirts of the city. "Something's not right," Bruce said. We stopped, looked at the map, and found we had followed it to a tea.

Assuming the concierge had given us good information, and eager to get a knockoff Chanel bag, Holly pleaded, "We're so close, Dad, we can't turn around now."

That's when, out of nowhere, a man wearing a hoodie and pants on the ground walked up to us and said, "Gucci, LV, Chanel, Coach, Prada." Taken aback for a moment, we thought, *This is a strange way to advertise, but yep, that's exactly what we were looking for*. Maybe our *I Love New York* attire gave us away. You think?

You might be thinking, *You guys are crazy,* and we would agree. We followed him into a warehouse as if we were under hypnosis, and before we knew it, we were in the service elevator with this complete stranger. It all happened so fast! Bruce and I looked at each other and immediately knew we had gotten ourselves into a real mess. The question, how will we get out — or . . . will we?

As we got off the dimly lit elevator, we followed him down a hallway. Now one guy was in front of us and another behind us. He opened a door and there were boxes and boxes of purses. The place was a mess and a sense of fear was upon us. Bruce stood in the hall, praying they wouldn't shut the door. He discreetly sent a text to a friend that said, "The girls and I are in New York. If you don't hear back from us in 15 minutes, call the police." He gave him the address we had been given and the name of our hotel. Trying not to panic, you can imagine what was going through his mind.

The two men were standing right there with us as we looked through the cardboard boxes. "Girls, find one you want so we're not late to our next stop," Bruce said, giving Holly *the look*. At 16, she was clueless to our surroundings. All she saw were designer bags, hundreds of them, at affordable prices. After about ten minutes (which felt more like hours), Bruce said, "Holly, isn't that the one you were looking for?" By then she too realized we might be in danger. "Yes! This is the one I wanted!" she said as she lifted a Chanel bag from the box.

After Bruce paid the man, he directed us to the stairs. I'll never forget the thoughts that flooded my mind as we walked down those five floors of stairs. The men, six of them now, stared at us the whole way down. With the exit in sight, we wanted to run, but we calmly walked through the door and made a beeline back to the hotel where we asked the concierge, "What in the world were you thinking?" Mortified that she had sent us, after some research, she discovered the place she referred us to had been closed down for weeks.

The next day, we heard police had raided the building. Later we found out that selling and buying a knockoff is against the law and sometimes the money is used to support terrorists and other crimes. Needless to say, we never used those purses.

As I thought about what had happened, the Holy Spirit brought to mind the story in Mark 7. Jesus called the Pharisees and religious scholars hypocrites (fake). "These people honor me with their lips [pointing to the religious people], but their hearts are far from me. Their worship is a farce, for they teach man-made ideas as commands from God" (vv. 6–7, NLT). *Farce* is the key word here. Fake. Counterfeit.

When I consider the lengths we went to get a designer look-alike, a knockoff, something that has no value, I cringe. Like the Pharisees and religious scholars wanted others to see their stature, did we really think that knockoff purses would go unnoticed? If it's not the real thing, it's a fake — period! To think some are seeking an imitation, a cheaper version, a look-alike to attain eternal security — that's scary! Jesus Christ is the way, the truth, and the life; He is the real thing. Obvious fakes may be skipped over, but many settle for a knockoff version of religion which in the end will cost them dearly.

Today there are hypocrites (fakes) in the church. They know what to say and when to say it, even how. They pull out the Jesus attitude when they can benefit from it. They are sly, and unfortunately their chameleon lifestyle turns people away from the church. With a check in her spirit and discernment in her heart, the real Christian can easily spot a fake from a mile away.

Then there are the knockoffs. They talk the talk and appear to walk the walk. But really, they dance around the idea of Christianity and never commit. The knockoff Christian is nothing more than a shell. On the outside she looks like the real thing, but her heart reflects self, not Jesus. She's constantly searching for something to fill her need. She goes from one thing to the next; she's never satisfied. The knockoff wants others to recognize her as someone important, or a good Christian, yet her heart is far from the Lord. The tragedy is that she believes her good deeds are good enough and will surely gain her entrance to heaven. In John 10, Jesus says,

> "I tell you the truth, anyone who sneaks over the wall of a sheepfold, rather than going through the gate, must surely be a thief and a robber! But the one who enters through the gate is the shepherd of the sheep. The gatekeeper opens the gate for him, and the sheep recognize his voice and come to him. He calls his own

sheep by name and leads them out. After he has gathered his own flock, he walks ahead of them, and they follow him because they know his voice. They won't follow a stranger; they will run from him because they don't know his voice"
(vv. 1–5, NLT).

A knockoff is like those who try to slip in through the backdoor, or hope because they look the part the right person will let them in. Isn't it sad that many searching for eternal hope, peace, security, and unconditional love get the wrong directions, only to find a temporary solution or a counterfeit?

In John 10:27 – 28, Jesus says, "My sheep listen to my voice; I know them, and they follow me. I give them eternal life, and they shall never perish; no one will snatch them out of my hand." What a beautiful picture of the real Church Lady. She knows Jesus personally. Her heart's desire is to reflect Him in her thoughts, actions, and words. She loves. She serves. She prays. She listens. She gives. She messes up. She repents. She's forgiven. She's humble. She's forgiving. She encourages. She is generous. She invites people into her home. She is happy for the success of others. She is genuine. She is the real thing!

Honestly, when I read Romans 12:20, I wanted to skip over it. "Lord, I don't have any enemies, so what can I possibly write that applies to this verse? And can Church Ladies reading this book really identify with 'serving your enemy'? And besides, the title of this chapter is *The Real Thing*! And what does that have to do with Romans 12:20?"

I looked up synonyms for *enemy* and found *rival*, someone who causes opposition and seems to be against us. Oh goodness! Now this is certainly something every Church Lady can relate to. That's when I was reminded of a personal story, a time when the Holy Spirit said, "OK, Chandra, if you really love with a genuine love, here's your chance to show it — *to your brother.*"

> *If anyone claims, "I am living in the light," but hates a Christian brother or sister, that person is still living in darkness. Anyone who loves another brother or sister is living in the light and does not cause others to stumble.*
> (1 John 2:9–10 NLT)

For many years, my brother Ronald and I had a strained relationship. I'll always remember one particular weekend when our simmering tensions erupted. I said some things that were definitely unloving and could have caused him to stumble. What we'd planned to be a wonderful family weekend ended rather quickly after Ronald and I got into a horrible fight.

Let me back up and give you some insight on our strained relationship. My brother and I (he's four years older) had not gotten along for years. We normally didn't fight; we just didn't speak. He had this way of intimidating everyone, especially me. It was common knowledge to family and friends that he didn't like me. He also thought that it was stupid (I can still hear him say those words), that I was so involved in church, and that Bruce and I had Christian values that we actually lived by. He felt that I thought I was so much better than everyone else.

After years of trying to be the nice sister, walking on eggshells at Christmas and other family gatherings, it happened! Like a steaming pot of water boiling on a stovetop, I guess you could say, the whistle finally blew! I'm sad to say now that it was ugly. He called me names and was very critical of me. I screamed back ugly things at him. Then I said some things that I regret to this day. Our family weekend was over before it had ever begun.

Years passed, and we saw each other at Christmas, but it wasn't very enjoyable, to say the least. Even when our dad passed away, this elephant was in the room. For years I'd prayed, "Lord, what can I do? How can I serve and love You and have such love for Your people yet have a brother who just might hate me?" Through the years, there was always a dull pain in my heart. Being in youth ministry, I was blessed to have a few godly men step into that brother role, but still I longed for my real brother to love me. I shared my hurt with close friends, and they too prayed for my brother and asked that someday God would restore our relationship. Ronald and I didn't see each other often, only when it was absolutely necessary. We would nod as each other entered a room and occasionally say hello.

One day when I was praying for my brother and his family, I know the Lord spoke to me. I opened my Bible and knew I'd found what I'd been searching for all these years.

Dear friends, since God loved us that much, we surely ought to love each other. No one has ever seen God. But if we love each other, God lives in us, and his love is brought to full expression in us. (1 John 4:11–12, NLT)

That was it! As I read this passage, my eyes filled with tears. I could see the pain of Jesus on the Cross dying for my sin. Then clearly my heavenly Father said: *I did this for you because I love you. And I did this for your brother because I love him. Surely you ought to love each other.*

In that moment everything changed — my perspective, my heart. Finally I had a fresh desire to love my brother for who he is. My brother is the daredevil of the family. His passion in life is going fast, jumping high, and entertaining large crowds! My love naturally expressed in words and hugs to others would need to be expressed through actions to Ronald. God was preparing me for what happened months later.

We got a call late one evening that Ronald had been in a serious motorcycle accident. Ronald had been racing in an arena when his glove somehow got caught on the throttle, a lever that causes the bike to speed up. While jumping from one hill to the next, he instead went straight up in the air and quickly straight down. He landed on his feet, which jammed everything up like an accordion into his pelvis area. Both legs were badly broken, his pelvis and other body parts were in a mess. The doctors were saying he was very lucky not to be paralyzed. However, he would need to be off his feet for at least a year.

By the next morning, Ronald had come through emergency surgery in which the doctors had replaced many broken bones with pins and metal bars. He was in pretty bad shape.

"What do we do?" I asked Bruce.

"Well, you need to go," he replied.

Knowing my relationship with my brother was strained, my dear friend Leslie rode along with me to the hospital. We prayed for my brother, his wife and kids, and especially that I would have the right words to say to a brother with whom I hadn't had a real conversation in years.

Not long after we arrived, I was able to go into the intensive care unit. He had tubes coming out everywhere and was still on a breathing machine. He couldn't speak because of the tubes down his throat — I couldn't speak because my heart was in mine. Then my mouth opened and words began to come out. It's not important what I said that day, but when he tried to talk back, he choked on the tubes. Bells started ringing, nurses came running, and they made us leave the room. I couldn't believe it! What had I said that made him angry? I pretty much ran to the waiting room, got Leslie, and ran to the car. On the way home I cried as I went over and over what I had said and questioned how those few words could have upset him so badly. As we drove those three hours back home, my dear friend remarked that if I couldn't talk to my brother, then maybe this was the time I should minister to his family by talking to his wife. I thought about what she had said and it seemed right in my heart.

The next morning my mom called me. Knowing I had been upset, she too was hurting for both Ronald and me. Then she shared with me how as soon as they took the tubes out of Ronald's mouth that morning, the first thing he said was, "I think I hurt Chandra's feelings." I started to cry. My mom began to explain that he had been resting there unable to speak, but had been thinking about exactly what I was telling him. He choked trying to respond back to me. Thankfully, what I said had not made him angry.

Isn't that just like Satan? Getting in the way of what God is doing? And this was going to be big!

Feeling much better, I called his wife, Teresa. We talked more in those next six weeks than we had in ten years. She was able to cry with me and share things with me during those days that brought us closer than ever. The healing had begun, both in Ronald's physical body and within my heart and his.

Weeks later while praying for my brother, the Holy Spirit nudged me to call him. I did and we talked for 20 minutes. That was a miracle! Over the following weeks while he was stuck in bed, we talked at least twice a week. Bruce and I prayed and asked the Lord to show us how we could minister to my brother and his family. Ronald would be off work for close to a year. We were obedient, and we gave what God told us to give. They needed financial support, and God had made a way for us to help. Instead of words, God prompted us to give just as He had prepared me to.

About eight weeks after the accident while on my way to an event, again the Holy Spirit tugged at my heart to call my brother. So I did. He was bored and had nothing to do and nowhere to go. Funny how God did that. We talked for 45 minutes. We laughed, talked about our dad (for the first time since he had passed away), and acted like brother and sister. We talked about his monster truck and motocross riding, things he enjoyed doing. Before the conversation was finished, he asked how my ministry was going. Amazing! We both agreed that this had been a great conversation and admitted that we were being real with each other. Ronald said, "That's the thing, I am who I am, don't try to change me."

"And I am who I am, so don't try to change me," I said. We laughed and agreed. It may seem like a little thing, but once we agreed to accept each other for who we are, everything else seemed to fade away.

Much to my surprise, we have more in common than I ever thought. Not the racing part of course, but the people part — we both love being with people! Wait a minute, that's not the best part of the story. On this day, I witnessed another miracle. I ended the conversation by saying, "I love you, Ronald, and I'm so glad you are getting better." And he said, "I love you too and thanks for everything y'all have done for us." Miraculous! Do you still believe in miracles? I sure do!

Can you spot a fake purse? It's hard to tell the difference sometimes, right? Oh that we might reflect the realness of Christ and never be mistaken for a fake. Be the real you and reflect the real Jesus to the real world. And when the Holy Spirit prompts you to do something, do it!

CAN I STAY WITH YOU?

On this journey in search of the Church Lady, God has interwoven the stories of others with my life experience. Recently a Church Lady approached me after an event. She said, "Romans 12:2 is the theme verse for our ministry, and like you, it is my prayer that women will come to understand this message: 'Do not conform any longer to the pattern of this world, but be transformed by the renewing of your mind. Then you will be able to test and approve what God's will is — His good, pleasing, and perfect will'."

She then introduced me to six ladies who were living at the Buried Treasures Home. Then she shared her precious story with me. Now I have the privilege to share it with you.

For years Nicki had a deep burden to tell women in the local jail about the love of Christ. Nicki looked into the eyes of each lady, placed a small chocolate candy called a Treasure into her hand and said, "You are a treasure, and I thank God for you." She knew that each lady was a rare and beautiful jewel to Christ and she wanted to be sure that they knew too. In 1999, after ministering to these women, one day a woman who was being released called Nicki and said, "I'm being released from jail but I have no place to go." Nicki and her husband, Dick Benz, prayed and brought her into their home. This began Buried Treasures Home. Today this woman is sober, has a job, and has a restored relationship with her family members who once saw her as hopeless. She is a treasured daughter, sister, mother, and friend, thanks to the grace of God and the opportunity to learn Godly principles from living at Buried Treasures Home. Today, Buried Treasures is a one-year haven of restoration and recovery for ladies who give their lives to Christ and seek His will as they discover that they are truly treasures in God's kingdom here on earth.

Dick and Nicki Benz have made all of this happen by sacrificially giving of their own lives. They have opened their home to more than 60 ladies, giving shelter, food, godly counsel, and direction for godly living.

These incarcerated women were not Nicki's enemies but they were strangers who Nicki welcomed into her home. Nicki Benz is a Church Lady. Her love is genuine. She is the real thing!

BUILD IT AND THEY WILL COME

When Hailey, my cousin's 15-year-old daughter, was admitted to MD Anderson in Houston, Texas, and diagnosed with a cancerous brain tumor, the news was devastating to say the least! If you have been through a major medical crisis, or know someone who has, you know we don't get to put life on hold while the critical circumstance consumes our every thought. With their home three hours away, not only did Hailey's parents have the heartbreak of watching their child undergo painful medical procedures and a life-changing illness, they were faced with a smorgasbord of stress. *What about our teenage son back home? Where will we stay? Will our employer allow us to miss work? How can we afford the added expense of parking, gas, food, and most importantly, what can we do to assure our daughter is happy, healthy, and whole?*

Before surgery, they stayed in our home for a couple of weeks, but the drive back and forth to the hospital (in Houston traffic) was excruciating for Hailey. Someone we knew graciously stepped in and rented them an apartment within a mile of the hospital for a month. Such generosity, such genuine love from people they had never met. Grateful but speechless, they began to see God's provision. With each obstacle, the Lord ushered in the answer and provided their every need.

After all the tests and recovery from surgery, Hailey needed extensive chemo and radiation therapy. Again, the question: *where will we stay and how can we afford it?*

We'll never know how far-reaching the request to pray for Hailey and her family spread, but we do know God heard the prayers of His people. A couple days before Hailey would be released from the hospital, her former minister of youth read her blog and realized she and her family needed a place to stay. Now the student minister at a church in Houston, he knew a couple who had moved close to the medical center whose ministry is to open their home for patients. After one call, they had a place to stay. Not just a place, but a beautiful home where the love and kindness of Christ was evident the moment they entered. And God's timing . . . perfect! The person who had been staying with them was moving out the very day Hailey was being released from the hospital. God had connected the dots and linked all these people together to provide for Hailey and her family. Our God is real and ever present in our lives.

In Ephesians 3:14–16 (NLT), Paul writes,

> *"When I think of the wisdom and scope of God's plan, I fall to my knees and pray to the Father, the Creator of everything in heaven and on earth. I pray that from his glorious, unlimited resources he will give you mighty inner strength through his Holy Spirit."*

Renée Heathcott was an only child. When her elderly and ailing parents needed assistance, she hoped they would move to Houston so she could care for them. However, they preferred to live in a retirement home in their own community in Oregon. After making countless trips to visit, there were times she simply couldn't make the trip. Realizing she needed a backup plan, she made her request known. While others eagerly filled the gap, Renée had a peace of mind. Grateful for the help she received, the Lord began to give her a desire to help others in their time of need, especially those who were from out of town. It was obvious — the Lord had used the kindness of others to prepare the Heathcotts for their next season of life.

After her parents passed away and she retired from her church staff position, she and her husband Ed wanted to move closer into the city to an area where Ed had grown up and where they had attended church when they first married. Ed sold a business he had and they were blessed to have a lump sum of money. This would afford them to buy a lot and build a home in this now-prestigious area of Houston, just minutes from the medical center. It's important to note that they weren't moving to this area for prestige, but the Lord was leading them there because He had a bigger plan.

God was at work and the Heathcotts were prepared. God's plan began to unfold. While working with the architect, it was clear they were to design their new home to be suitable for guests with medical needs. Because the lot size in this neighborhood was narrow, the house would be two stories. One side of the second story would be built with adequate privacy for the comfort of guests. An elevator would be needed and grab bars in the bathrooms. As she shared her story with me, I thought of Noah: with no sign of rain, he built the ark and paid close attention to every detail because God told him it was going to flood, and it did (Genesis 6:11–22). The Heathcotts also heard from the Lord. They too paid close attention to every detail to assure the needs of critically ill patients. The Lord said to build it and they will come, and they did.

In fact, just after they moved in, while putting the finishing touches to their home, they got a phone call. A minister of youth and his wife from Crockett, Texas, had a crisis pregnancy and needed to be within 20 minutes of the medical center immediately.

They arrived soon after the invitation was extended, and this was the beginning of their open-door ministry. The Heathcotts enjoyed this couple, and as they awaited the birth of the child, they began to love them like family. Seven weeks after they had arrived, their precious baby was born, and it seemed as though the Heathcotts were adding a new member to their family.

The Lord continues to fill the guest quarters with out-of-town patients who need shelter. Most are cancer patients; however, one was a heart transplant patient who stayed with them for two months. Not able to climb stairs, he was very thankful for that elevator!

The Heathcotts are the real thing. Renée is a precious Church Lady who has the gift of hospitality and has graciously opened her home. The Lord gave the vision, supplied their every need, and the Heathcotts have been blessed, as they are a blessing to others.

ARE YOU THE REAL THING?

Oh the joy of being the real thing, knowing that it is He that has called you for a purpose and is giving you everything you need to fulfill that purpose. Is there anything better than obedience to our heavenly Father? What a sweet spot!

Perhaps the Lord is calling you to do something. Does anything come to mind? Is the Holy Spirit beginning a new work in you? If so, get excited and hold on! Believe me, if the Lord is asking you to do something, He's already prepared you for the task and you'll never regret your obedience.

If asked to give to your enemy financially, will you? If someone needs shelter, will you open your door? And if someone needs a mentor, a spiritual teacher to help them grow in this marvelous faith, will you step up to the plate? If someone needs a fresh start, will you encourage and believe in that person? When people see you, is it obvious that you are the *real thing*? "Then you will be able to test and approve what God's will is — his good, pleasing and perfect will" (Romans 12:2).

Reveal and Transform

The first and most important message of the chapter: don't be led astray, Jesus is the *real thing*! Just like we were in search of knockoff designer bags, many people are in search of a savior. Jesus Christ is the only One who can satisfy us, the only One who will fill that empty place within us. His grace, love, acceptance, forgiveness, and salvation are available to all who will accept Him as Lord and Savior. Many get off course and fall into dangerous paths. They need Church Ladies like you and me to live out the Christian life, to be genuine — the real thing.

1. How do you treat someone who opposes or comes against you? Giving or doing for this person is not on the top of your to-do list, I would guess. Have you ever had the urge to help a *hard-to-love person*? If so, did the Lord give you the desire to follow through? What was the outcome, or is it something you're working towards?

2. Do you have a hard-to-love person in your family? Ask the Lord to help them see that you are the real thing and that your love for them is genuine.

3. "Do not conform any longer to the pattern of this world, but be transformed by the renewing of your mind. Then you will be able to test and approve what God's will is — His good, pleasing, and perfect will" (Romans 12:2). In this very moment, how does this verse apply to your life?

4. Have you ever missed an opportunity because you didn't trust the Lord? God asked Nicki to do something BIG, and not only has she been blessed by her obedience, but she has witnessed the transformation of women. Is God calling you to *do something BIGGER than you?* Explain.

5. "If your enemies are hungry, feed them. If they are thirsty, give them something to drink. [Conquer] evil by doing good" (Romans 12:20-21, NLT).

Ponder this Scripture. Could the simple gift of food and drink really change a person? I believe it can. I think there is more to this Scripture than the food and drink. Your thoughts?

CHAPTER 14

The Garden Within Your Heart

Don't let evil conquer you, but conquer evil by doing good.

— ROMANS 12:21 (NLT)

Imagine you're walking on a path through a grassy field and you see a beautiful gate surrounded by large yellow sunflowers. Curious, your steps become stronger, your stride a little longer. You realize the path leads to a garden. The fragrance of honeysuckle draws you in. In the silence, you hear the flutter of hummingbird wings. You smile as you watch the colorful, tiny birds dip their long dainty beaks into the center of beautiful pink flowers — cockleshells, you quickly recall. Your sense of smell is on high alert as a sweet aroma of honeysuckle fills the air. You distinguish between familiar flowers and those you can't identify. Hearing a bird sing a twee-dilly-tweet, you turn in that direction and notice a red bird perched on top a birdhouse that resembles a church. You notice a bench farther down the path, so you slowly make your way. The warm sun and the gentle breeze brush against your face as you stretch your arms across the bench and tilt your head back. In the serenity of this sacred moment, everything within you gives thanks and praise to God, the One who created it all. In the stillness you sense His presence, and everything on that to-do list fades away. You feel a sense of peace and tranquility as you bask in His marvelous love. The Master Gardener cleanses you and fills you without speaking a word.

I come to the garden alone as the dew is still on the roses . . . are the words of a familiar hymn. As we give to and nurture others, meeting with Him is essential, not only for how we respond and react to others, but for how we live our lives!

After enjoying a beautiful bouquet of fragrant flowers for only a few days, I was shocked when I noticed they were wilted. The vase was white, so I couldn't see inside, but when I took a look, it was completely dry! Seriously! It didn't even appear wet. I immediately filled the vase with water, and by that evening the flowers were standing tall again.

Could this describe your week — your life? We can't see our spiritual gauge (inside our heart), but our actions and attitude are a tell-all sign when our spiritual fuel tank is running on low. Talk to any woman and she can relate. Her current season of life determines her daily routine. If she has young children, her routine looks very different from the woman in midlife whose children are leaving the nest, or the grandmother who spoils her grandchildren before sending them back home, the woman who is caring for her elderly parents, the other for her ailing husband, or the widow who after rocking babies in the church nursery sits home alone. Oh the seasons of life — like swinging doors, they usher in such change.

While the gift of nurturing is a blessing from God, the Church Lady often neglects caring for herself. She is notorious for spinning one plate too many. As she pours out, her energy quickly runs out. To experience *being* rather than *doing* sounds delightful, but who has time for that? Frankly, being still is hard with so much on her *to-do* list, and even Bible study can seem like *just another chore*.

True, if Satan can't make the Church Lady bad, he'll sure make her busy. Can I get an *amen*? How many times have we answered with a quick yes when we certainly should have said no? Throughout Scripture we are taught to love God first and then love others. And certainly serving others is the best way to demonstrate our love. While our motives are good, spreading ourselves thin can lead to unforeseen trouble. Satan is crafty. He uses the busyness of plate-spinning to keep us from spending time with the Father.

So where is the balance?

Jesus gives us a beautiful analogy in John 15:1: "I am the true vine, and my Father is the gardener." The balance is easy when we are connected and stay close to the vine (Jesus). You've seen it, I'm sure: a branch on a rose bush, long and lanky with a teeny tiny bud on the end. Prune that limb back and before long a larger bud grows, sure to produce a beautiful, fragrant rose. This same description can be said of godly women who are connected to the vine yet doing life according to *your name*.

The solution for the frazzled plate-spinning woman: sit and be still in the presence of the Master Gardener. Even Jesus went alone to the garden to pray in His most desperate hour (Matthew 26:36–46). Away from the crowds and the disciples, in the solitude, He spoke with His Father and He heard from His Father.

Where is your place of serenity?

I enjoy gardening . . . when I have time. The moment I see specks of green unearth from the warmth of the ground, and splashes of color begin to sprout like paint on a tapestry, my green thumbs become enlightened. God's unveiling of all things new assures change outside and inside too!

Like a child I flip through gardening magazines, looking for the prettiest pictures, hoping to find inspiration. A few years ago I had a plan and I was off to the local garden center. After pulling a cart from the front of the store, a gentleman wearing a bright orange vest greeted me with a smile. "Can I help you?"

As I said, "Yes," I noticed his name tag. Bob — master gardener. *Just the person I was looking for,* I thought. "I want to plant pansies and I want them to look just like this (pointing to a torn-out picture from the magazine)."

He smiled. "Yes, ma'am. The problem is people come in hoping to achieve this look but they don't take the time to make it happen. Gardening is a process. The most important step is to prepare the soil."

I listened intently as he shared seven steps to a healthy garden:

1. Pull out any trash, clay, or old roots to ensure the new roots will grow deep and strong!
2. Get rid of insects, being sure there are no slugs or snails. They will eat the roots before the plants ever have a chance.
3. Till the dirt — mix in cow manure and fertilizer, being sure the soil is soft, ready for new growth.
4. Plant the pansies three inches apart and three inches deep.
5. Mulch the area. This will hold moisture and protect the plants from heat.
6. Water and apply a bloom booster to ensure new growth and full blooms.
7. Wait and watch them grow.

As he loaded the supplies in my basket he said, "You also need the right tools." He threw in a three-pronged tilling tool, a small shovel, and pink gloves. I wondered how he knew I'd like the pink ones. "Now go forth and plant."

I got right to it and was determined to follow his instructions. As I finished, several neighbors stopped and commented on the beautiful pansies as I proudly sprayed them with my new long-handled soft-watering tool.

A couple weeks later when I returned from an out-of-town event, I was disillusioned by what I saw — or maybe what I didn't see is a better account. More than half of the flowers were petal-less. Hundreds of worms were dining on the petals. That's right — they were eating them! As I got closer, I watched as one of the worms devoured an entire petal! I was appalled as its cheeks became the size of a small marble. The prettiest garden I had ever planted, and poof, overnight, gone, destroyed!

I immediately went to see Bob the gardener. He was calm — I was not. His expertise gave me some hope. He assured me that with quick action and proper care, the pansies would bloom again. As I followed him down the aisle he said, "Worms can wipe out a garden in less than 24 hours. You need to spray insecticide to eliminate them. Repeat the process again tomorrow. Some will die right away, but there are always a few stubborn ones in the bunch. Then clip off the dead growth and spray the bloom booster on them again. In a week or two, your garden will be exploding with colorful blooms again."

As I sprayed those worms, I was reminded of the words of Jesus in John 10:10: "The thief comes to steal, kill, and destroy. But my purpose is to give life in all its fullness." And in 1 Peter 5:8: "The enemy prowls around like a roaring lion looking for someone to devour." This enemy was a worm and he certainly did some major damage.

Our heart is the garden within. "As water reflects the face, so one's life reflects the heart" (Proverbs 27:19). Therefore, we need to guard our heart from evil and ask the Master Gardener to tend our garden continuously. Why? Because when life is going well, we let our guard down. And as quickly as those worms attacked my garden, Satan can attack our heart in a single moment. Satan comes to destroy us when and where we least expect him.

What a great illustration the worms give us. It didn't matter that I did everything right. I prepared the soil, fertilized, watered, sprayed the flowers with bloom booster, but still the worms came. Church Ladies, don't let your guard down! Don't think just because you are trying to do good, evil will not bite at your heels.

Jesus instructs us to stay close to the true vine (Jesus) and let the Master Gardener tend to our heart. Then the branches (believers) will be fruitful. When we stay close to the vine, we reap the blessings of His life-giving power. We stay alert and have the strength to fight off Satan's attack — not if — when it comes.

When was the last time Satan slithered into your environment? You know how he is in those gardens. Maybe instead of forbidden fruit or worms he used trash from your past to stop new growth. Perhaps he planted seeds of lust to keep your focus off things and on those thorns of resentment who keep people you love at a distance. Unfortunately those thorns are entangled with briars so thick that if not cut down, they will leave your heart dry and cracked, empty and broken. Can you see why we need to take time to meet with Him? Only the Master Gardener can pull out those weeds that shadow your inner beauty and remove the briars that choke out new life. His love is greater than our mistakes. When we sit with the Master Gardener, He cleanses and purifies our heart. Take time to sit under the shade and take comfort in His love today.

And I pray that you, being rooted and established in love, may have power, together with all the Lord's holy people, to grasp how wide and long and high and deep is the love of Christ. (Ephesians 3:17–18)

NEED PRUNING?

Every time I hear the word *pruning* I think of my daddy. He pruned the crepe myrtle trees every February. I asked him why he cut them so much. He explained that by cutting them back, they would grow larger and more beautiful in the spring. I never understood how that worked, but every spring, sure enough, the pink puff balls showed off their splendor once again. We are keeping that tradition, and every February I think of what my daddy and what my heavenly Father told me. Jesus says, "I am the true vine, and my Father is the Gardener. He cuts off every branch on me that bears no fruit, while every branch that does bear fruit he prunes so that it will be even more fruitful" (John 15:1–2).

Spiritual pruning — seasons of suffering and refining — can be painful, but it is always for our best. Like a loving father disciplines his children, the Master Gardener prunes us to keep us in step with His plan, to make us stronger, and to prepare us for the job He has for each of us to do.

Remember, apart from the vine, the branch cannot bear fruit; apart from Jesus, we can do nothing (John 15:5).

PULLING WEEDS

Chances are, in our spiritual emptiness and complacency, we will begin to meddle in the gardens of others — judging what they have planted (do wrong), upset by the weeds (sin) in their garden. Funny how we are quick to notice the weeds growing in someone else's garden while weeds are growing in our own.

Have you ever had someone finger-point at your sin? Not a good idea. Instead, women of God should love one another unconditionally. Finger-pointing at the others' sins is not our job. The Holy Spirit nudges us to repent of sin, then Jesus heals and forgives, cleanses and purifies. The cry of *create in me a pure heart, Oh God* (Psalm 51:10) needs to come from the heart, not the timing of a nosey neighbor or another Church Lady. So while we are made to nurture and counsel, we must recognize that others' hearts are not our responsibility.

A note for mothers and wives (I am both): Although we want to *fix it* or *fix those* we love, we can't. We can pray for them, love them, and give them godly advice, but ultimately we make our own choices. Life is a process. Although it is difficult to watch those we love suffer, we need to trust the Lord. Remember, obedience brings blessings. Disobedience blocks blessing (Deuteronomy 28). There are consequences for disobedience, and we can't change a person on the inside — only God can.

FEELING SPIRITUALLY EMPTY?

Where can we get a refill, be restored and replenished? When we are connected to the true vine (Jesus), we allow the Master Gardener (God our Father) to tend to the garden within our heart continually. When we are parched both physically and spiritually, Jesus shouts, "Let anyone who is thirsty come to me and drink. Whoever believes in me, as Scripture has said, rivers of living water will flow from within them" (John 7:37–38).

Flowers get parched by heat, broken by wind, but then the rain comes and once again the blooms lift their heads to the sun. When our heart is broken and bruised, the living water is like healing rain, washing over us, cleansing and purifying us. As a result, we lift our heads in thanks and praise to the Son. Perhaps this, too, is part of the process that makes us more like Him.

The LORD will guide you always; he will satisfy your needs in a sun-scorched land and will strengthen your frame. You will be like a well-watered garden, like a spring whose waters never fail. (Isaiah 58:11)

THE MASTER GARDENER CONTINUOUSLY TENDS TO HIS GARDEN

When I was in Vienna touring a castle, the beauty and perfection of the gardens took my breath away. Several acres were impeccably groomed. The tour guide explained that the gardens are divided into sections, each having its own gardener. She explained to us that each of those gardeners report to the master gardener.

"He is the boss," she said. "He has the blueprints of the gardens and he knows the names of each shrub, tree, and flower planted throughout the garden. He walks the gardens every day to assure timely pruning, trimming, and grooming, and watering and fertilizing is achieved. He inspects the garden down to the tiniest details. Slugs and bugs seldom do damage because the master gardener knows when even one thing is out of place. He doesn't just have a green thumb, he has a green heart." She laughed. "The only thing he can't supply is the sun."

Oh sister, did you ever consider that our hearts compare to a garden in so many ways?

THE SECRET GARDEN

Perhaps you are familiar with Frances Hodgson Burnett's *The Secret Garden.* Rich with biblical symbolisms, it was my favorite reading assignment in high school. If you are not familiar with this classic novel, allow me to give you a very short digest. After the sudden death of his wife, the heartbroken rich uncle closed off the garden which she had adored. He buried the key and had forbidden entrance to the garden. Years later young Mary, his niece, came to live with him after a cholera epidemic killed her parents. After befriending the uncle's difficult hypochondriac son and a servant's brother, Dickon, they found a key and discovered a door in a wall. As they pushed the door open, they realized it had once been a beautiful garden, dry, dead, and overgrown. They began to tend to the garden. They pruned the dead limbs, pulled weeds, cut the briars, and watered the garden. Over time the garden began to burst with vivid, fragrant blooms of color, and the lush garden was restored.

Like the rich uncle, we too allow hurt, bitterness, and _fill in the blank_ to keep us cut off from the abundance the Master Gardener has planned for us. We choose to shut the door and throw away the key, and deal with our pain in secret. The Bible tells us that nothing in all creation can hide from Him (Hebrews 4:13).

Pain, discontent, and hurt feelings become the thorns in our lives that keep others away — those we love most, those who care the most about us. I've seen so many failed relationships (friendships, families, and marriages) because with bursting emotions came ugly words. Satan loves this! When we create our own mess, he steps back and smiles.

The danger of a Church Lady with a hurting heart is that she is likely to hurt others. Soon the garden within her will wither up, and although she is alive, she is not living and surely not joyful. There is no chance of this happening when we are intertwined with the True Vine. He is our source of strength, regardless of our circumstances, and our joy in every circumstance comes from Him.

And if Satan has you believing you're withered up and good for nothing . . . au contraire! Like the garden, the love of Jesus can bring you back to life, fill you with joy, and you'll be in full bloom before you know it.

The Master Gardener replaces our human flaws with the fruit of the Spirit: love, joy, peace, long-suffering, kindness, goodness, faithfulness, gentleness, self-control. Now we are full. We can love, give, and serve. We can conquer evil by doing good because we have obeyed Him and remained in His love. He tells us this so we will be filled with joy to overflowing (John 15:9–11).

We Church Ladies are like flowers. There are hundreds of petals in the garden, but no two are exactly the same. And when you and I are planted in the firm foundation of Jesus Christ, we can't help but bloom into the beautiful, unique, one-of-a-kind woman our Father created us to become.

If only we would sit and be still for a while with the Master Gardener, allow Him to pull out weeds, till the soil, plant, water, and pour on the bloom booster, then we would be ready when He sends us out to the frontlines, doing the business He created us to do. Only then can we discover the freedom to be the woman of God He designed us to be. Only then can we genuinely love others. Only then can we conquer evil by doing good (Romans 12:21).

WAITING FOR GROWTH

Patience is a big factor when planting a garden. The gardener will surely experience frustration and pain between the planting season and the harvest season. When I consider the hurtful and painful experiences in my own life, I can testify that there was spiritual growth and always a grateful heart on the other side of heartache. The Master Gardener knows all and sees all because He is the creator of all. Be encouraged!

In the drive-through mentality of our generation, we get instant gratification most of the time. So in our rush to satisfy our wants, we often jump ahead of God. Could it be that His amazing and merciful love allows stumbling blocks to slow us down and road blocks to get us back on His track? God's plan for us is far greater than anything we can imagine (Ephesians 3:20). If we are in a relationship with Him first, He lavishes His favor on those who genuinely love and surrender their lives to Him. And like flowers after the rain, we lift our heads to the Son, and we thank Him for His timely provision.

So when the worms come, stay strong and be confident that the Master Gardener is at work. Put *Spending time with the Master Gardener* at the top of your to-do list, or . . . just keep spinning all those plates. The choice is yours.

When we remain in Him, He remains in us and we will produce good fruit. This, sweet sister, is how we conquer evil. I pray this encourages you to sit in the garden more often with your heavenly Father, the Master Gardener of your heart and mine.

But they delight in the law of the LORD, meditating on it day and night. They are like trees planted along the riverbank, bearing fruit each season. Their leaves never wither, and they prosper in all they do." (Psalm 1:2–3, NLT)

May this become the prayer of every Church Lady as we do good in the sight of the Lord.

REVEAL AND TRANSFORM

1. A tall plant like a tomato plant needs support to grow and produce good fruit. We too need support, to lean on others (a friend, family member, daughter, mother, sister in Christ) as we go through the challenges and celebrations of life (grief, sorrow, pain, joy, weddings, births, death, and disappointment). Make a list of events when you needed the support of another.

   a.

   b.

   c.

   d.

   e.

2. Doors — I've always enjoyed taking pictures of beautiful doors and antique gates; they mysteriously capture my interest. Doors have such meaning. Consider the doors you have walked through and the doors of opportunity that are yet to be revealed. The life of a Church Lady is exciting, as we never know what door He will open next. And my favorite connection with doors is that in Revelation 3:20 — Jesus stands at the door and knocks. He invites us to open the door. When we do, He comes in. Have you opened the door of your heart to Jesus Christ?

   - *Above all else guard your heart. Why? Because it affects everything we do* (Proverbs 4:23).

3. What kind of garden is growing in your heart? A garden filled with love enough to share with others? A heart of bitterness and discontent? Maybe you have decided to plant fruit trees that will produce a peaceful heart, joy, and the desire to help and serve others.

THE GATE

Bruce and I were on a cruise for our 15th wedding anniversary with two other couples. When our ship docked in Barbados, we had planned our own excursion and hoped to find a beautiful beach off the beaten path. Be careful what you wish for.

While renting a van for the day, we asked the man behind the counter if he could tell us where to find what we were looking for. He smiled, shook his head, and said, "Don't worry. Be happy!" His map was easy to follow until we made a right turn onto what seemed to be private property. A little concerned, we noticed a sign was there just like he had drawn on the map. So we turned in, and the road quickly became a dirt road. With a trail of dust behind us, we began to think the native had possibly led us down a road to nowhere. Anxiety rushed in when we saw cows with rings in their noses chained to a ring on the ground. Four out of six of us suggested we turn around. One of the husbands said, "I don't know about this. Three ladies, three men, tourists. Who knows? This could be a set up. We could be driving straight ..."

"Wait," I said as I pointed. "Look! There are some wrought-iron gates."

That's when we all agreed to continue on the path, and then out of nowhere he appeared: a man well-dressed in all white — white hat, white pants, and a white shirt.

"Welcome, guests."

Steve asked, "Is this the way to the beach?"

"Yes, yes. Don't worry. Be happy." We all laughed.

We drove through the gates and some of the guys were still a bit leery. "Just go!" the rest of us agreed. That's when we saw it — the most beautiful sight I have ever seen! We had no idea that we were at the edge of a cliff just before we made a sharp left turn. Wow! Steve stopped the van, and for a moment, we were a bit shocked at what was right in front of us. We were high on a cliff and could see for miles out to sea. The colors were brilliant, defined, like lines separating the deep navy blue from the deep turquoise, then the green ending with light turquoise like a backyard pool; it seemed to be a rainbow of blues. The waves were hitting against the black lava rock, sending a splash of white into the air which rested against the perfect baby-blue sky. As we looked down to the beach, the pure white sand was dotted with bright-colored umbrellas that seemed to be calling our names. "Paradise!" we all agreed.

Once again reflecting back on the trip, the Lord revealed another truth from this picturesque snapshot in my mind: so many believers never experience the fullness of God, nor the abundant life that He desires for those who love Him, because they live in fear. That day we had to take some risk. We had to make a choice and put a little effort into the planning. We could have settled for the most popular beach, but we took a risk; we stepped out in faith that we would find that beautiful beach. We had a map, we had directions, but along the journey, doubt and fear crept into our minds. We had a choice to make: turn around or keep going.

Thankfully, after a little hesitation, we continued on the path that had been laid out before us. We almost turned around at the gate — but we didn't. We drove through. We could have decided to turn around just past the gate. We certainly couldn't see the view just past the gate. No, we had to keep going. We had to trust that our directions led us to our destination. Once we made the decision to go for it . . . there it was. In my mind's file under Beautiful Places, this one tops them all.

Applying that to your Christian walk, has fear kept you from experiencing all that God has planned for you? Have you missed blessings along the journey? Perhaps you've had an opportunity, but you let people talk you out of it while in your own heart you felt it really was the thing you should do. And then you might just be one who has entered the gate, but you're still holding onto it. You know you are going to heaven, and isn't that enough? No! God the Master Gardener has so much more for you to experience, so much more for you to see and to do. There is so much more to being a Christian than just the ticket that gives you entrance into the pearly gates, and you can experience it here on earth.

Jesus says, "Yes, I am the gate. Those who come in through me will be saved. Wherever they go, they will find green pastures" (John 10:9).

What is the condition of your heart today? Open your gate wide to the Master Gardener. If you choose to invite Him in, the transformation will be astounding — talk about a beautiful garden! He will plant flowers, trees, fruit, and greenery you never knew existed!

REVIEW AND TRANSFORM

*Therefore if anyone is in Christ he is a new creation; the old has gone,
the new has come!* (2 Corinthians 5:17).

*For God, who said, "Let light shine out of darkness," made his light shine in our hearts
to give us the light of the knowledge of the glory of God in the face of Christ*
(2 Corinthians 4:6).

Write your thoughts.

CHAPTER 15

Jumping for Jesus

s I sit here in my office, ready to write this final chapter, my mind has spontaneously begun flipping through the files of my mind. What an amazing journey it has been! The tear in my eye is bittersweet. More times than I can count, I've opened the *Church Lady* file, saved it on the hard drive of this my third computer since that first night I saw her. As I look back, it's clear. The connections have been perfectly timed to His orchestrated plan. Again, I trust Him for the inspiration, to give the words to share as I press on with the completion of this manuscript. With confidence, I trust He will have the final word before He wraps the ribbon around this work and ties a beautiful bow of His approval on top.

Now that the end has come, I wonder if this is just the beginning of a God-sized opportunity, or the closing of one door and the opening of another. When I consider these chapter titles have been laid out for eight years, I shake my head in wonder — He who gave me the outline knew all those years ago the path I would take to collect each story to fit perfectly with the title. I've prayed, waited, and thought surely the Holy Spirit would nudge me to change one here or there, but no. Instead I'm persuaded to keep that which He has given me from the beginning.

In fact, the title of this chapter comes from a particular story from years ago. Think back to the 80s and 90s when I taught aerobics at a studio, and after a few requests, a class at my church too. I'm laughing out loud as I remember the pink tights, purple leotard, and matching hair bow that sat on top of my high ponytail. Oh goodness, then there were those high-top Reeboks and parachute pants. Thankfully Lindsey and Holly were too young to remember, but I'm sure the girls at Spring Memorial Baptist Church can picture it. Can you?

My husband, Bruce, has worked for a wonderful Jewish family since 1982. An employee of the same company got married at our church, and the Steins were among the guests at the wedding. I remember how excited we were to have them in our church. Walking through the fellowship hall after the wedding, Mr. Stein noticed an advertisement for my aerobics class. He said, "Well, isn't that special. Chandra Peele — *jumping for Jesus.*" For years now, every time I see him, the first thing he asks is, "Are you still jumping for Jesus?" There's just something about it every time I hear this loving Jewish man, who I have prayed for all these years, say the name of Jesus. What a privilege to respond, "Yes, sir! I'm still jumping for Jesus." These three words remind me that God is glorified even when His daughters work out with a choreographed routine to Steven Curtis Chapman's "Saddle Up Your Horses." Funny, isn't it, how all these little things weave their way into God's big plan?

Years later while preparing to teach on the power of God in Acts 3 of the New Testament, I realized the crippled beggar jumped for Jesus too. It's a story of a man, lame from birth, who was placed at the gate called Beautiful every day as worshippers went into the Temple. Now that I've actually visited the Temple area in Jerusalem, saw what people call the Beautiful gate, and sat on the steps myself, I have a vivid picture. Imagine, every day the same routine — lying there, shaking his beggar's cup back and forth, hoping someone would throw in their pocket change. But on this day, God had a better plan. God was ready to change his life and give him what he really needed — to be healed. When Peter and John passed by the man, Peter got his attention when he said, "Look at us!" The exclamation point is as important as the words. God uses exclamation points to get our attention, to help us snap out of our routine. Perhaps He's used a few in your life, circumstances that got your attention.

Peter took him by the right hand and helped him to his feet. The man's feet and ankle bones became strong and the crippled man was healed! In verses 8—10 of the text,

> "He jumped to his feet and began to walk. Then he went with them into the temple courts, walking and jumping, and praising God. When all the people saw

him walking and praising God, they recognized him as the same man who used to sit begging at the temple gate called Beautiful, and they were filled with wonder and amazement at what had happened to him."

REVIEW

- He had a handicap. So do we.
- He had a daily routine. So do we.
- He hoped for enough to get by on. So do we.
- He almost missed what God was doing because he was distracted. We too get distracted.
- The man looked up and lifted his hand. We need to do the same.
- The power of God healed the man. God still performs miracles today.
- People noticed he was leaping and jumping and praising God and they recognized him. People are watching us.

THE POWER OF CHRIST IN YOU

Church Ladies, it wasn't Peter or John who healed this man — it was the power of God who healed him. However, Peter was the willing vessel God used to heal the man. Today God is looking for obedience in us, Church Ladies who are willing to be vessels, ready to go when He says *go*. His power flowing through you will be just what is needed to accomplish His purpose.

On the other hand, you may be going through a difficult season and you relate to the crippled beggar — handicapped, broken, beaten down, perhaps stuck in a rut you can't escape. Have faith in your season of weakness. If someone comes along to help, let them. In your weakness and humility, God is strong and powerful!

Your circumstance, good or bad, does not define you. God does.

As you've read the stories in this book, surely you've remembered those who have touched your life — who God used to serve, teach, and shape you. As you remember and give thanks for these people, don't forget to give thanks to God. Don't forget to *jump for Jesus*!

Jumping for Jesus is simply a term of endearment given to me by a sweet Jewish man named Bruce Stein. Let these three words remind you to do something outwardly that shows your uninhibited love for God. Think about it. When the woman at the well ran to tell others that she saw Jesus, the Messiah, people were changed because of her excitement. When Jesus fed over 5,000 with five small barley loaves and two fish, people were astonished and began to say, "Surely this is the Prophet who is to come into the world." When Jesus calmed the sea and walked on the water, when He forgave the adulterous woman, when He healed the blind man, when He healed ten men with leprosy, changed the heart of a dishonest tax collector named Zacchaeus, and miracle after miracle, we know about it today because of what people said or did. When the risen Jesus appeared to Mary Magdalene in the tomb, He appeared to Mary — a woman — first! He said, "Mary. Do not hold onto me, for I have not yet returned to the Father. Go instead to my brothers and tell them, I am returning to my Father and your Father, to my God and your God" (John 20:17). Mary Magdalene did as Jesus told her. She ran to tell the disciples! Can you imagine her excitement? I imagine her kicking off her shoes, picking up the hem of her robe, and running as fast as she could to tell the disciples. She couldn't contain her excitement! For generations past and every generation to come people, will be changed because on that day, Mary Magdalene proclaimed that Jesus was not dead — He is alive!

TAKE THE CHALLENGE

When God does something in your life, get in the habit of telling others. It may be the very story God wants to use to connect the dots; to light the path of another, so they too can experience this life-changing salvation.

NOT NOW, PLEASE!

While I was writing this book, I was interrupted with a phone call from my brother-in-law. Short and to the point, he told me they really needed my help selecting paint colors for their house. (FYI — I enjoy decorating homes when I'm not speaking or writing.) Immediately I thought, *Are you serious? Could the timing be any worse? I really don't have time for this. I'm working on a deadline, here.* But the word *yes* seem to roll off my tongue as if I had no control. The next day I drove to their home (45 minutes away) and made the paint selections.

One thing led to another and before I left, I had agreed to redecorate their house while they were out of the country for three weeks. As soon as I got in my car, I said, *Lord, what just happened here? I don't have time to take on this huge project!*

They left on their trip, and when the painters had completed their job, I went over to see what I needed to begin mine. The paint was beautiful, but the house was a mess — disorganized, to say the least. Overwhelmed, I didn't know where to begin. I realized this project was much bigger than I could possibly take on. I got the nerve to send an email to explain why I could not do the job. After getting the message, my brother-in-law called via Skype. While I gave him every excuse I could think of, he said, "Hey, don't worry about it. Melanie (his wife) will be disappointed, but she'll have to understand." Later that evening I got another Skype call — this time it was Melanie. She was truly regretful, and I heard despair in her voice. As she tearfully shared her story, I realized the trials and heartache she had experienced during the past year. God began to transform my heart, and His love and compassion won out. The next day I went back to their home, and while standing in the midst of a house that looked as if it had been turned upside down, the Lord said, "Chandra, you are going to do this because I need you to help Melanie." So, I did. I knew He was at work because this huge inconvenience was now turning into a driven desire to complete the task.

He gave me the will to do my best, and I did. Only by the grace of God did I have time to shop for new items, find a cleaning crew and some men to move furniture, to complete the makeover, *and* meet my book deadline — all in two weeks. When He dropped this unexpected task in my life, everything in the natural said *no way!* But with His power at work within me, I was amazed at what we (the Lord and I) accomplished.

Ready to unveil the makeover, I went over early, lit a few candles, turned on all the lamps, and assured everything was in place before they arrived. The moment Melanie walked through the door, it was all worth it! I'm not sure what God is doing in Melanie's life, but I know somehow in His perfect plan He used me to help.

We all have a handicap. Melanie's was depression. It was holding her captive, sucking the life and joy right out of her. She was truly stuck in the miry muck of bad circumstances and she needed someone to help her.

What is your handicap, the thing that keeps you from living life with joy, from experiencing the freedom you have in Christ Jesus?

Paul writes,

"For by the grace given me I say to every one of you: Do not think of yourself more highly than you ought, but rather think of yourself with sober judgment, in accordance with the faith God has distributed to each of you. For just as each of us has one body with many members, and these members do not all have the same function, so in Christ we, though many, form one body, and each member belongs to all the others. We have different gifts, according to the grace given to each of us. If your gift is prophesying, then prophesy in accordance with your faith; if it is serving, then serve; if it is teaching, then teach; if it is to encourage, then give encouragement; if it is giving, then give generously; if it is to lead, do it diligently; if it is to show mercy, do it cheerfully" (Romans 12:3–8).

Whatever you enjoy and are gifted to do, do it for the glory of God. If the Holy Spirit nudges you to do something, don't allow negative thoughts to heap feelings of inadequacy on you. Instead, know your self worth, your identity in Christ, and be confident that He has made you capable for the job at hand. When we make ourselves available, God's love through us is contagious! And we may never know how significant our influence is on the people we serve.

I'm no biblical scholar; I'm just an ordinary girl who loves Jesus! That exclamation point belongs there, I promise. God has inspired me to encourage you, woman of God, and Church Ladies all over the world to find freedom in a life surrendered to Him alone; to remind you that in most cases it's not in our success that He changes us, challenges us, and creates in us an excitement to share His amazing love, but instead it is in our failures, flaws, and fatigue where we glory in His glory.

When you recognize true freedom in Christ, as I have experienced during this journey, you really will have a bounce, maybe even a jump in your step. Don't settle for the pocket change this world throws your way. God wants to give you what you really need — abundant life overflowing with joy — no matter your circumstance. Believe me, He can and He will.

Today there are Church Ladies all over the world living with shame, guilt, past hurts, depression, or perhaps they are in a funk, therefore living with a handicap — a life of mediocrity. As my dear Christian brother David Nasser says, "I can't take no mo'!" Choose to lift your head and your hand — like that beggar on the temple steps, discover His power in you. Then go and tell someone what He has done for you.

The Lord used Bruce Stein, a Jewish friend, to resonate in me the far-reaching influence we have when we jump for Jesus. As with Melanie, I don't know what the Lord is doing in the life of Bruce Stein, but I know He's doing something God-sized!

As my fingers strike these keys, I'm praying the joy overflowing from my heart will supernaturally spill over to yours. I pray the words on these pages have made an impact on your life, encouraged you, changed you, caused a check in your spirit, made you want to tell someone that you love and appreciate them, and most of all, that you have a new excitement to live out the Christian life; to consider it an honor to be a Church Lady. How exciting to imagine Church Ladies around the world finding freedom to be who God has called them to be. Who have been changed from the inside out, ready to go when opportunity presents itself. Who are recognized to the world as His body — His hands and His feet — serving, loving, giving, encouraging, teaching, reaching, and *jumping*, all in the name of Jesus.

I don't know what the Lord is doing in your life, but I know for sure He's doing something!

REVEAL AND TRANSFORM

The Word of God never returns void, meaning it always speaks to the heart that's open and powerful enough to touch the heart that is closed. Although I believe each story in this book was given to me to share with you, I am confident that nothing speaks more clearly than the Bible, His holy inspired Word. To assure this book makes an impression on your heart, I would ask that you read the Word below and open your heart to hear what the Lord is speaking to you today.

> *You yourself are a case study of the mighty hand of God. The mystery in a nutshell is just this: Christ is in you; therefore you can look forward to sharing in God's glory. It's that simple. That is the substance of our Message. We preach Christ, warning people not to add to the Message. We teach in a spirit of profound common sense so that we can bring each person to maturity. To be mature is to be basic. Christ! No more, no less. (Colossians 1:21, 26–28, The Message)*

Mark's Gospel emphasizes Christ's power as well as his servanthood. Jesus's life and teaching turn the world upside down. The world sees power as a way to gain control over others. But Jesus, with all authority and power in heaven and earth, chose to serve others. He held children in His arms, healed the sick, washed the disciples' feet, and died for the sins of the world. Following Jesus means receiving this same power to serve. As believers, we are called to be servants of Christ. As Christ served, so we are to serve. (Mark 16:20 NIV)

Luke's Gospel portrays Jesus as the perfect example of a life lived according to God's plan. As Christ followers today, we should look to His example, live our life according to His plan, study the Word of God, and share the good news, so others can be restored through salvation.

Jesus tells John, "Feed my sheep. Follow me!" (John 21:18–19). There it is again, an exclamation point.

1. What do you say about Jesus?
2. Do you read and study His Word?
3. Are you feeding His sheep?
4. Are you an obedient follower of Christ?
5. Will you serve others even when it's inconvenient?
6. When He opens a door for you to serve, do you trust Him to supply the need and to equip you for the job?

If you want to reflect Jesus Christ to the world, start by serving just one. Serve wholeheartedly, with a genuine love and with excellence.

Church Lady,
The power of Christ is in you.
Be confident and live in His power!
His light is in you. Shine in the darkness!
When it seems like an inconvenience, trust that
He will work all things out for His glory.

Conclusion

Precious Church Lady, what a privilege it has been to share these stories with you, to encourage you in the name of Jesus. In the Book of Colossians, the words of Paul, inspired by God, give rich wisdom for Christian living. In the first chapter he speaks of forgiveness and encourages believers that if Christ has forgiven us, then we should forgive others. Forgiveness is a big deal! How ironic that one of the greatest struggles we face is forgiving when God sent His own Son to die so that we might be forgiven. If you are harboring hurt or are bound by an unforgiving heart, forgive today.

My favorite discovery in this chapter — there is no secret plan. The mystery has been revealed with the coming of Christ. The greatest story ever told, the greatest treasure ever found is "Christ in you, the hope of glory" (Colossians 1:27). To know that God, the Creator of all, planned for Jesus Christ to live in the hearts of all who believe — it's priceless! He is the Answer! He is your Answer!

Church Lady, let it be said of us that we are unified as we carry out the cause of Christ.

> My purpose is that they may be encouraged in heart and united in love, so that they may have the full riches of complete understanding, in order that they may know the mystery of God, namely, Christ, in whom are hidden all the treasures of wisdom and knowledge. (Colossians 2:2–3)

In chapter 3, Paul encourages us to set our minds on things above, not on earthly things. Now, this would certainly change our perspective on all kinds of things, wouldn't you agree? When we regard the temporary things of this life, perhaps our choices, our words, and our actions would reflect Him more.

I want to thank those who have prayed for me through the years, my friends and Church Ladies all over the globe who have given me the opportunity to share my journey. Surely you will understand why there are tissues sprawled all over my desk as tears of adoration roll from my eyes — and yes, snot from my nose — when you see how perfectly the Holy Spirit puts the final period on this project. The only thing that could make this moment more special is to have you here with me, to celebrate what God has given me the privilege to do; the stories, some of them yours, for His glory. How precious that He has led me to these verses. He is indeed the author and finisher of all things.

Therefore, as God's chosen people, holy and dearly loved, clothe yourselves with compassion, kindness, humility, gentleness and patience. Bear with each other and forgive one another if any of you has a grievance against someone. Forgive as the Lord forgave you. And over all these virtues put on love, which binds them all together in perfect unity.

Let the peace of Christ rule in your hearts, since as members of one body you were called to peace. And be thankful. Let the message of Christ dwell among you richly as you teach and admonish one another with all wisdom through psalms, hymns, and songs from the Spirit, singing to God with gratitude in your hearts. And whatever you do, whether in word or deed, do it all in the name of the Lord Jesus, giving thanks to God the Father through him.

(Colossians 3:12–17)

Can you see her? The lady dressed in purple, singing praises in the vision? And where is it that we usually sing in unity? The church. And who are the people singing? The church. And who is that beautiful woman of God, the one who has been set free? It's you! The Church Lady.

Publish his glorious deeds among the nations. Tell everyone about the amazing things he does. Great is the Lord! He is most worthy of praise!

(1 Chronicles 16:24–25 NLT)

Use the QR reader on your
smartphone to visit us online at
www.newhopedigital.com

If you've been blessed by this book, we would like to hear your story.
The publisher and author welcome your comments and
suggestions at: newhopereader@wmu.org.

Additional resources for Women by New Hope Publishers

God, Grace, and Girlfriends
Adventures in Faith & Friendship
Mary R. Snyder
ISBN-13: 978-1-59669-326-5 • $16.99

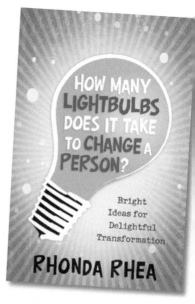

How Many Lightbulbs Does It Take
to Change a Person?
Bright Ideas for Delightful Transformation
Rhonda Rhea
ISBN-13: 978-1-59669-325-8 • $14.99

Available in bookstores everywhere.

For information about these books or any New Hope product,
visit www.newhopedigital.com.